Endorsements

The author of this book describes a family's reliance on and trust in the Lord as they walked through the Valley of Baca. The book gives hope, comfort, and understanding to all who read it. Heartily recommended.

- Albert H Oosterhoff, LLM
Professor Emeritus
Western University (Law)

In this sober, moving account John van Popta tells the story of the illness of his son Julian, and of the way of bravery, despair, resilience and exhaustion Julian, his parents, family and friends had to go. It is a story of pain and encouragement, medical accomplishments and incapacity, of joy and lament. At crucial moments, God does not seem to respond to calls for help. Yet in all the weeping, hope – even beyond death – becomes real in relationships.

- Koert van Bekkum, PhD.
Professor of Old Testament
Evangelische Theologische Faculteit
Theologische Universiteit Kampen | Utrecht

God calls most of his people to pass through dark valleys. Few valleys are deeper, and few are darker than the ones in which we see our children suffer. This is a book that will be a blessing to all of those who are being called into times of suffering, sorrow, and uncertainty.

- Tim Challies
Author, Seasons of Sorrow

Heartbreaking and hopeful, these raw, unedited emails record the van Popta family's journey through the valley of the shadow of death and the Good Shepherd's often mysterious presence and care. It was a privilege to be Pastor John van Popta's friend and colleague in the next town over during these events, and to read these emails as they first appeared. I am delighted to see them available to a wider audience.

- John Barach, M.Div.
Minister of the Word
Covenant Presbyterian Church
Sulphur, Louisiana

This is the story of a family's heart-breaking journey through the valley of the shadow of death. It will almost certainly make you weep. But it will also lead you to worship the God whose grace is sufficient, and whose goodness and mercy in Christ follow us all the days of our lives.

- William den Hollander, Ph.D.
Professor of New Testament
Canadian Reformed Theological Seminary

"Julian has been diagnosed with leukemia." I remember exactly where I was when I took Pastor John's phone call that late summer afternoon. The news came like a thunderbolt, shaking the basement where I was standing. Julian's remarkable story, so lovingly detailed in this journal, is an encouragement to all. This book is a must-read and is already a best seller in my heart.

- Peter Buist, Ph.D.
Professor of Chemistry Emeritus
Charleton University

This collection of journal entries is vivid in its attention to medical detail and gripping in its stream-of-consciousness style, but what makes it especially worthwhile is its compelling testimony to God's sovereignty and love.

- Jannes Smith, Ph.D.
Professor of Old Testament
Canadian Reformed Theological Seminary

Though it is autobiographical, this book deals with such deep experience that it becomes archetypal. Much can be written about it, but at minimum John van Popta's account of his pilgrimage through the valley of Baca gives us a fleeting glimpse of the infinite love of the Father who gave up his Son for us.

- Daniel Shin, B.A., M.Div.
Minister of the Word
Spring Creek CaRC
Vineland, Ontario

Only When It's Dark Can We See the Stars

Only When It's Dark Can We See the Stars

A Father's Journal as His Son Battles Cancer

John van Popta

> **Library and Archives Canada Cataloguing in Publication**
>
> Title: Only when it's dark can we see the stars : a father's journal as his son battles cancer / John van Popta.
> Names: Van Popta, John, author.
> Identifiers: Canadiana 20250214083 | ISBN 9781069370204 (softcover)
> Subjects: LCSH: Van Popta, John—Family. | LCSH: Parents of cancer patients—Canada—Biography. | LCSH: Parents of cancer patients—Religious life. | LCSH: Leukemia in children—Canada. | LCSH: Fathers and sons,—Canada—Biography. | LCSH: Cancer—Religious aspects—Christianity. | LCGFT: Autobiographies.
> Classification: LCC BV4910.9 .V36 2025 | DDC 248.8/6,—dc23

Only When It's Dark Can We See the Stars:
A Father's Journal as His Son Battles Cancer
Copyright © 2025 John van Popta
Providence Books & Press
All rights reserved

Brief quotations from this resource may be used with conventional acknowledgments in presentations, articles, and books. For all other uses, please write Providence Books & Press for permission.

Any descriptions of treatments and their providers are solely from the personal perspective of the author. The names of medical personnel have been changed to preserve their anonymity.

Scripture citations are from the Holy Bible, New International Version®, NIV®. Copyright © 1973, 1978, 1984 by Biblica, Inc.™ Used by permission of Zondervan. www.zondervan.com. The "NIV" and "New International Version" are trademarks registered in the United States Patent and Trademark Office by Biblica, Inc.™ All rights reserved.

ISBN: 978-1-0693702-0-4

 Box 3 Site 15 RR2
Barrhead, AB
T7N 1N3

Dedication

I dedicate this book to my loving wife, Bonita;
my fellow Pilgrim through this vale of tears,
who by her gracious care and prayer,
has supported me for nearly 45 years.
And to Julian's brothers and sister.

We all suffered and sympathized
together with Julian on his journey
and our characters were formed
by these events in our lives,
more than we know.

Contents

Foreword 13
Prologue 15

Chapter One
From Where Does My Help Come? *Days 1-25* 17

Chapter Two
He Will Not Let Your Foot Slip: *Days 27-161* 47

Chapter Three
The Lord Will Keep You: *Days 240-910* 85

Chapter Four
In the Shadow of Death: *Day 1021-PSCT Day 39* 121

Chapter Five
Through the Valley of Tears: 155*PSCT Days 55-85* 155

Chapter Six
From Strength to Strength: *PSCT Days 140-434* 169

Chapter Seven
Awaiting the Final Day 185

Postscript 191

Foreword

My nephew, Julian van Popta, was diagnosed with a serious illness, Acute Lymphocytic Leukemia (ALL). The treatments are brutal in that the patient is brought to the brink of death.

In this book, made up of his journal posts, Julian's father, John, describes the journey the family traveled. The pilgrimage passed through times of fears and tears, and periods of rest and relief. Julian and his family were encouraged by two loving clans, countless faithful friends, several Christian congregations, and innumerable doctors, nurses, and other medical staff.

Above all they were helped along the journey by their heavenly Father.

As a pastor, my brother John has been called upon to help many families struggling with illness and disease. But now it was their own son. Illness stopped at their door and visited the family for several years.

It is difficult for the patient, but it is also excruciating for parents and siblings. My own immediate family has been spared serious illness, so I can only imagine how hard it would be to see one's child deathly ill. As believers we confess that life and death are in the hands of our faithful, loving, heavenly Father.

By whom will this book be appreciated? I would say by all who read it. It will be valued by those who, themselves, have endured ALL, or another serious illness; by their parents and family; and by anyone who, in one way or another, has a loved one battling such hardship.

Many children die because of grave illness or disease, but we should never despair. As Christians we have a living hope. We are all on the pilgrimage, traveling — as John alludes — through the Baca Valley. This valley is mentioned in Psalm 84 and describes reliance on God for strength during hardship, tells of the longing to be with God one day in his sanctuary, and reminds us of blessings that we will there enjoy.

Listing many of our Old Testament brothers and sisters, together with whom we are trekking towards the better country, Hebrews 11 assures, "Therefore, God is not ashamed to be called their God, for he has prepared a city for them."

Take up and read, and be encouraged!

- George van Popta, B.A., M.Div.
Minister of the Word, Emeritus

Prologue

In late August 1996 we noticed that our 12-year-old son Julian was not feeling well. He suffered from general malaise and lethargy. We would find him napping while his brothers played outside. His stamina had faded. Working for a market gardener in the heat of an Eastern Ontario August drained him completely before noon. He developed inexplicable bone pain. Our family doctor decided that a tender arm was tendinitis (though he doubted his own diagnosis). Julian lost his appetite; his eyes and face got puffy. On Wednesday, August 28 the doctor ordered a complete blood count. This was done the next morning. Our family physician called us on Friday:

> All Julian's blood counts are low. Do you understand what that might mean? I have set up an appointment for you at the Medical Day Unit at CHEO (Children's Hospital of Eastern Ontario). You must go there immediately. This morning. They will be waiting for you.

John van Popta

Our lives have not been the same since.

Before the day (August 30) was out, we were confronted with childhood cancer. Julian was diagnosed with Acute Lymphocytic Leukemia. Chemotherapy was to begin the next day. Some of the first moments of those days stand out, cut from crystal in my mind, amidst the confusing blur of activity. Julian was admitted to the oncology ward at CHEO. There we met the first of very many professionals who would make up Julian's care team.

This journal was written as e-mail postings, first of all to family and friends. After the first week I began posting them to an Internet electronic mailing list, REFNET, primarily made up of members of Reformed and Presbyterian churches around the world.

In the past I had seen children suffering from childhood cancer but had no idea of the challenges the families faced. I hope that my semi-regular postings helped others appreciate the physical, emotional and spiritual battle Christian families face when childhood cancer strikes. I trust that this book will do the same.

Though in the pilgrim's journey there are many difficult days, only when it's dark can we see the stars.

Chapter One

From Where Does My Help Come?

Days 1-25

Day 1

Dear Family and Friends

As some of you know, and others do not, our middle son Julian (12 years old, going on 13) has been diagnosed with Acute Lymphocytic Leukemia. He is a patient at the Children's Hospital of Eastern Ontario (CHEO). He was diagnosed yesterday, Friday afternoon (August 30, 1996). This morning he underwent surgery to "install" a "port-o-cath." This is a small stainless-steel chamber, which is placed under the skin in his upper chest area. A catheter connects the chamber to a major vein. Through this chamber and catheter, the various medicines will be administered for the next months and years.

Julian is in relatively good spirits but he is frightened about all this. He knows that cancer is a terrible illness and knows that the treatments will not be pleasant. He is also in protective isolation on the oncology (cancer) ward. He may not come out of his room to spend time with other patients though he may have visitors - family and friends. We are on Day One of a long journey.

Bonita and I and the rest of the family, along with Julian are slowly coming to grips with this. I suppose that it will be some days before the reality sets in.

We continue to trust in the Lord

John & Bonita

Day 2

Dear family and friends

Today we worshipped the Lord with our congregation in Ottawa. The elders led the services and I was able to sit with Bonita and the children. It was very difficult for us this morning, but we were comforted by the Gospel. An elder read a sermon prepared by Rev. G. van Popta (my brother and the former pastor in Ottawa) on the marriage feast in Cana. The Lord Jesus by turning the water in the stone jars into wine shows that he removes the pinched and strained purity of the Pharisees and replaces it with abundant - super abundant - joy. The Lord Jesus does not work in half measures! He removes completely the sorrow brought on by sin and the brokenness of this world. He gives us reason to celebrate and to experience true and deep joy.

These are words our family needed today.

Julian was in good spirits today. He rested well. Towards evening however, his first bout of nausea took command of his body. He looked and felt miserable. Julian's ever-present smile was in short supply tonight. We have received support from many friends and are encouraged by the willingness of many to share our burden. It is, however, so difficult to share in Julian's personal sorrow and fear. He is a very frightened 12-year-old. We noticed today that he is having a very difficult time responding to all these new situations. It is as if he has no learned responses. He speaks little and has great difficulty articulating what he thinks or feels.

We cannot imagine the thoughts going through his head. Mention of the word "cancer" strikes fear in all men's hearts; what does it do to a young fellow?

The staff is very concerned that their patients understand their situation. They encourage him to ask questions and be involved in the processes (and there are many).

They are also very straightforward.

He was issued a high-quality baseball cap on his admission to 4-East. "Does this mean I will lose my hair?" "Yes it does, Julian." "Not me! I'm not going bald!" This was within two hours of his diagnosis.

Only When It's Dark

It is late now. I need some sleep. Thank you for your prayers and email.

john & bonita, Julian, and his siblings.

Day 3

Dear family and friends

Julian felt awful today. His chemotherapy is killing off the immature white blood cells that have invaded his organs and other systems. The cells, as they die off, release uric acid and other toxins. These toxins cause terrible nausea. With Gravol, Demerol and other anti-nausea drugs they manage to keep him relatively comfortable though this active young man does not like being bed ridden. Bikes are to be ridden, not beds! Dr. Hasper, the oncologist, assures us that the nausea will relent in a day or three as the kidneys purge the toxins from the body. During that time, the Demerol will keep him in a semi-conscious state. He drifts in and out of sleep and can hardly speak three words. I lay my head on his bed and wept before the Lord as he slept.

The ward has been very quiet since Friday. The other children had been sent home for the Labor Day long weekend. Many will be drifting back in tomorrow and Wednesday. I think this too will impress upon us the full reality of Julian's condition. Today already we met some of the other patients and families and are hearing the stories of their battle with cancer.

Bonita and I are quickly learning all sorts of stuff about molecular biology, organic chemistry, and a host of related topics. Today we signed onto a research project in which the doctors are attempting to correlate blood iron levels and intakes to incidents of juvenile leukemia. Dr. Roland explained that she has shown how leukemic cells can only divide in the presence of iron. The cells consume vast amounts of iron and so leukemia patients, having their iron robbed by these "pirate" cells, become anemic. This has been shown in the lab - in the test tube, so to say. She now needs to gather data in the field. If it holds true in clinical study then one more small piece will fall into place in the complex puzzle called ALL.

We are encouraged by the support received from you all and know that your prayers are being answered in that we receive the strength to go on in the Lord.

Under the grace of God

john and bonita, Julian and the rest

Day 5

Dear Family and friends

Julian is eating again! (Amazing how quickly the perspective changes on such little things in life. A father gets excited that his 12-year-old eats breakfast!) He smiled and cracked some jokes today.

Thank you all for your words of encouragement, your calls and of course, your e-mail. We are printing out the e-mail and putting it in a binder for Julian.

Daily we live under the grace of God.

John & Bonita

Day 7

Dear Family and Friends

It has been one week since we learned of the cause of Julian's health problems. It seems an eternity.

Julian is in protective isolation because his immune system has been seriously compromised by his leukemia as well as by his chemotherapy. We receive daily sheets with his blood counts and are learning to read them. Some of his immune system counts are running at about 10% of a minimum acceptable level.

Julian is in excellent spirits today. He is on a drug - Prednisone - that boosts his appetite. He wakes up hungry. He needs snacks. He was laughing and joking today. It is my birthday, so we had a party in his hospital room - though two weeks ago we could not have imagined such a scene - Julian in bed hooked up to an IV, Mom, Dad, a sister and three brothers in their yellow gowns and yellow masks, having a birthday party! It was surreal! We had to laugh at the situation. Martin asking, "How are we going to eat this stuff!" as he tries to negotiate his jellybeans behind his mask.

Today was a "four drug day." Julian is on a full four-drug therapy for high-risk patients. These drugs are administered on different schedules: every day, every three days, every 8 days.... Today they all coincided. Some of these drugs, one especially, is very dangerous. It will take some time for the doctors to determine if he must continue to be treated as "high risk." He is considered high risk because of his age. The younger the better. However, there is also a process by which they can determine from the genetic makeup of his malignant blood cells if he is in a low, medium or high-risk category. When they combine that data with other factors such as age and severity of the disease, they may down grade him to a medium and so take him off some of the more dangerous drugs. Because of his age, he will not achieve a low-risk status.

His treatment is broken into three parts: induction (1 month), consolidation (11 months) and maintenance (18 months). The total protocol takes 130 weeks minimum and often stretches on to 150 weeks (149 to go!). With the Lord's blessings, Julian will be approaching 16 by the time his chemo ends! When I told him this he said, "I don't want to talk about that."

We checked with the hospital tonight just before I wrote this. His nausea has started again from today's treatment. They will call us in the night if he needs us. Pray for us.

Under the grace of God.

john, bonita, Julian and the rest

Day 10

Dear family and friends

Today marks ten days of living with leukemia. The reality of childhood cancer is sinking into our household. We are encouraged by the many telephone calls and by the cards and letters and notes that are beginning to arrive by post and e-mail. Living in the midst of the church of Jesus Christ and being lifted in prayer by the many saints of God is a source of great comfort and the source of what little strength we have. (I believe Lord, help my unbelief!) It is only at the throne of grace that we find mercy and grace to help in our time of need.

Julian has made it through his first four-drug treatment day with flying colors. The doctor says that he is "a good patient."

The treatments are progressing well. On this Thursday, September 12, he will undergo his most extensive treatment yet. He will receive two drugs orally, one drug intravenously, one drug inter-muscularly, undergo general anesthetic so that they can do a lumbar puncture whereby they remove fluid from around his spinal cord and brain and inject a three-drug mixture into the spinal fluid. They will also do a bone marrow aspiration whereby they remove bone marrow from his hip for analysis. This will be the only day in his one-month induction period that every drug and procedure of his protocol will be administered.

In addition to his Thursday's treatment, he regularly receives two types of antibiotics in his IV to fight off any opportunistic infection. Because one of his drugs is affecting his pancreas, Julian has gone temporarily diabetic. His blood sugar has begun to climb and today has gone very high. He is 'spilling' sugar into his urine. His kidneys are already taxed to the limit clearing all the uric acid from dying leukemic cells and all the other toxins that his liver is trying to metabolize. Dr. Louis called in the endocrinologist who has put him on twice daily insulin shots to control his sugar levels. This means that they need to draw a drop of blood from his fingers every 6 hours to monitor his sugar levels. They monitor every bit of fluid - water, juice, pop, milk, IV that enters his body and all the fluid that exits his body (they even measure his vomit! Ugh! We are glad for them that there is very little of that.) They also have given him platelets (a blood component) twice in the past few days, as well as a "whole-blood" transfusion. This was to alleviate his anemia as well as the low level of clotting ability of his blood. Julian has also told us that his vision is being affected. This morning he had trouble reading the time on the large clock in his room. We hope that this is because of his diabetes and not because of neural toxicity. We will know in a day or two.

Dr. Louis told us a ... "a parable" I suppose you could call it. "This battle with cancer is like your lawn which is full of weeds - choked with dandelions. You spray your lawn with very strong chemicals and the dandelions die. But this makes your lawn look terrible. It now has all sorts of bare and bald spots. It is, however, time to wait for the grass to grow. Your son's bone marrow is that lawn and it is choked with leukemic cells. We are going to kill them all! That is our aim. But along the way, he is going to look terrible. He will suffer nausea. He will lose his hair. He might go diabetic. He will be weak. He will shake, lose weight, get puffy. His eyesight may be affected. His liver and kidneys will be challenged to their very limit. His heart might be affected. But all of this is just the sideshow. We must kill the weeds ... and then wait for the grass to grow."

Dr. Louis goes on: "Don't be distracted by all the secondary effects. They are all manageable. We can do this or that. Insulin, diet, anti-emetics, antibiotics, Demerol, Gravol ... we have it all. We very (!) closely monitor and control his blood chemistry and other body functions. And we will do this so that we can get these powerful drugs into his body to attack the malignancy in his bones and to prevent that malignancy from getting into his central nervous system. His cancer is the only real enemy here. It is his cancer that we must defeat."

I cannot imagine hearing this and being parents who do not have the Lord God sustaining them through the grace of Jesus Christ.

Living under the mercy of God, seeking help at the throne of grace.

john & bonita, Julian and the rest

Day 13

Dear Family and friends of Julian

J ulian's treatment is in its 13th day. Technically it is "Day 15" for him but "Day 15" falls on a Saturday and "Day 15" of his "induction protocol" needs the expertise of doctors and anesthetists. The treatment schedule was moved up to today so that any complications and side effects will become apparent before Saturday, when less staff is on duty.

Julian's diabetes is proving to be a little difficult to control. At first, they thought that a little insulin would do it but now he must also control his diet.

He does this willingly realizing that he needs to help the doctors treat his illness and control the side effects. It seemed rather harsh though. Drugs like Prednisone make him hungry. Others affect his body's ability to use sugar. (I think someone once called diabetes "starvation in the midst of plenty.") Julian wakes up shaking like a leaf, he is so hungry. And then yesterday, we had to tell him that he could not eat breakfast today because of the anesthetic he would take for the other treatments. We were pleased that they were able to get him to day-surgery before lunch. The nurses had told him and his mom that he would likely feel awful and want to sleep when he came out of day-surgery. When they wheeled him out of the clinic, he was conscious, though groggy. As they brought him to his room his mother took his hand and squeezed it. Eyes closed, he squeezed back and whispered with a smile, "Where's breakfast?"

Tomorrow he will be rewarded with bacon and eggs - ordered up special, just for him!

The mail (lots of it!) that is coming from all over the world is a source of great joy for our son. He is encouraged by the gracious words and the knowledge that so many pray for him. He gets to open and read mail sent just to him and then sets it out for a day or two. From there he pastes it into a scrap book (to make room for new mail), along with the stickers the IV nurse gives him each time they come for blood or change his IV. (He has many stickers!) His arms are battered and blue. His blood does not clot very well so every time they puncture his veins, he gets a bruise on his arm or hand. For every bruise a sticker!

His 13th birthday is September 21. We do plan to have a birthday party for him!

Some friends were visiting this week - friends of his - and he was showing them "his" Super Nintendo, TV, VCR and mini-stereo as well as his cards, stickers, "Archies" and other goodies. One of his 11-year-old visitors exclaimed, "Way cool man! I wish I was in here!" to which Julian replied solemnly and simply, "No you don't! It's neat, but it's not worth it." Julian is fully aware that he is in a struggle for his life. He is in a titanic spiritual, emotional and physical struggle. This is the battle of his life. A friend noted today that he has grown up in two weeks; he has grown up more than anyone would wish his child to grow. Childlike naiveté evaporates in the face of death and yet he greets each day with a positive enthusiasm. He is cheered by each and every visitor who comes. He loves to share the goodies that, because of his diabetes, he may no longer eat. He is learning to read the smile in people's eyes (their lower face hidden by their yellow mask) and so smile in return. It took me some days to learn that he did not smile at anyone simply because he could not see their faces!

Julian had a special visitor yesterday. Marnie McBean (and two other rowers - Olympic athletes) came to CHEO to visit the children. Julian had heard about this from a nurse. He had understood that they would visit the ward. This turned out not to be so. He was so disappointed. So, the "Child Life" worker went up to talk to the PR people. Marnie McBean agreed to come to visit Julian in his room. She donned mask and gown and visited this young man. It made his day! He was able to handle her Gold Medal and she signed his scrapbook and the diary we are writing for him.

Bonita just called me from the hospital and told me that they had to give him one more drug - "the RED medicine" they call it - and then he will have had all his drugs for the day - all his drugs in one day! His nausea is beginning again. It all seems so cruel. The side effects are so visible... His hair will likely begin to fall out by early next week. His body shakes. His limbs are thinning. And the enemy so invisible! It would not be so hard to take these medicines myself, but to say to the doctors, "Go ahead, give that poison to my son" is a decision more difficult than I had ever imagined. Next time you see a child bald because of cancer treatments, think also of the staggering emotional battle the child's parents go through making life and death decisions. On one level it is very easy: "Go ahead, do what must be done!" on the other, "No, never! Don't you dare make my child vomit, or shake, or go bald or weep! Don't you dare give my son chemicals that will affect his heart and pancreas and liver and bones and nervous system!" Lord, have mercy on us!

And through all this, we find comfort in the Psalms. Together with Julian, we are walking in the valley of the shadow of death, but we fear no evil. We are not afraid! We tremble, but do not panic. We are in the Valley of Baca, the valley of tears. We weep, but do not mourn as others do. Our cup overflows, and goodness and mercy follow us every day, for we live in the presence of God and in the shelter of the Most High. We do not fear the pestilence that stalks the darkness, nor the plague that destroys at midday (Ps 91:6). "Dear Lord, do not be far from us, for trouble is near and there is no one to help (Ps 22:11)."

In the midst of all this, the Lord gives us the peace of mind to go on with our daily work. I am able to prepare sermons for Sunday; Bonita continues to teach the younger sons school and as a family we manage to live with hope and confidence for the future. This all, only by the grace of God conferred upon us through the prayers of the saints and by the saving work of Jesus Christ. In him alone is our hope and confidence.

john & bonita, Julian, lorien, christopher, reuben and martin

Day 17

Dear Family and Friends of Julian

Julian's treatment on Day 13 is taking its toll on this young man. Having three potent chemicals injected into his lower spine and having a bone marrow aspiration done on his hip three inches over from his spine left him unable to lay on his back or even sit up. The Prednisone, a catabolic steroid, (burns off living tissue) is causing him to lose weight. His drug induced diabetes is continuing to prove hard to manage. The L-asparaginase and Daunorubicin cause nausea and so he does not eat much. This in turn affects his weight and his blood sugar. The Prednisone also affects his moods. On Sunday, Julian had a hard time remaining cheerful.

Saturday, he began to experience great pain in his lower

bowels. The drugs that he receives are specific to swiftly multiplying cells. The body has swiftly dividing cells in hair follicles; hence the loss of hair. But there are also swiftly dividing cells in the mucus membranes and in the lining of the digestive system. Especially childhood cancer victims are susceptible to blisters, ulcers and lesions in the digestive system. It seems that Julian has developed sores in his lower bowels. One of the fears the doctors have, has occurred. These sores have become infected. The doctors, unable to immediately determine what sort of infection has invaded, have prescribed two powerful antibiotics and a new anti-fungal drug to be administered by his IV.

His pain is being managed by morphine injected straight into his blood stream through his chest catheter. When the doctor told Julian that he could receive something for pain, our 12-year-old immediately asked if it was going to be "that awful drug that made him feel so heavy. I don't want to sleep all the time!" He was referring to the Demerol he had last week. He would rather have terrible pain than that! The pain, however, was so bad that every breath he took elicited a moan. He even asked that his older brother and his friends not visit! When they administered the morphine, he had relief within two minutes! And he does not have this heavy groggy feeling from it. We thank the Lord for powerful drugs like morphine. The doctors say, "There is no need for our patients to suffer any serious pain."

We need to constantly remind ourselves that these complications are a "side show." The doctors are confident that they can manage all these side effects - that they can keep them from becoming life threatening - and so continue their assault on the deadly illness in his bone marrow.

I asked Dr. Louis today what his assessment of Julian's condition is. He said, "Oh, he has presented me with no challenges yet! Julian has is a 'garden variety' patient. Nothing unexpected. Just a few more side effects than average!" We were encouraged by that, though the thought that it could get much worse, and that it does for many patients and parents, is staggering. We are hoping that his blood counts will begin their slow rise back to normal this week.

There are times that we think of Julian as a big and living chemistry experiment! If you did this to a healthy child, you would be sent to prison! Being "home-schoolers," this should do as Julian's "Science and Health" unit for the fall term!

We were heartened that Julian was able to be free from his IV pole for an hour today and was allowed to walk the halls. He could not walk very quickly, and not without help, but he enjoyed his moment out of his isolation (though now he had to wear a mask and gown.) It is stunning that a child so strong and healthy can become so weak and ill in a matter of three weeks!

Our family, in the midst of this, continues to experience new mercies every morning. In Christ and in his suffering, we have hope and confidence for the future. God's grace is sufficient for us.

john & bonita - Julian - lorien, christopher, reuben, martin

Day 25

Dear Family and Friends of Julian

Twenty-five days! It seems a lifetime ago! Julian continues to live in protective isolation but is picking up day by day. His massive chemotherapy treatments have ended and now only continues to take one drug daily. His infection has been knocked down. His diabetic problem, however, remains a stubborn nuisance. That too, though, is straightening out. He no longer suffers from bouts of nausea.

We are hoping that his "blood counts" will be good enough by Friday for him to come out of isolation. Some time ago I had said that Dr. Louis compared the treatment to spreading chemicals on your lawn to kill the weeds and then waiting for the grass to grow. Well, we are in that waiting stage. As the effects of the powerful treatments taper off, Julian's bone marrow is once again beginning to produce the right kind of blood cells in the right ratios. Tomorrow he will undergo another bone marrow aspiration. A sample of bone marrow from his hip will be tested. It will need to be 100% malignancy free. There has to be complete and total remission, for the treatment to move on to the next stage - "consolidation."

On Friday or Monday, we will meet with the care team and discuss the results of this test as well as the genetic markers and evaluate his response to the treatments. This assessment and evaluation will be the time that decisions concerning future treatments will be made as well as what his prognosis is. These are truly tension filled days for us. In the next few days, we will find out if his treatments so far have been successful (95% of patients do go into full remission) and what his risk factors will be. So far, we have really only been able to get used to the idea of childhood cancer. In the next week we will have to plan (under the condition of James 4:15) Julian's and our next years as we learn to live with childhood cancer.

Julian is in good spirits and he is beginning to ask more questions about his illness and his future. He too is wondering about the 'what ifs?' He is encouraged by the well wishes that pour into his room via the mail room every day. Around his birthday (Sept. 21) Julian was getting between 15-25 pieces of mail per day! Virtually all the mail coming to his ward is for him. Someone asked if he was decorating his room with his mail! Actually, he is pasting the hundreds of cards into a large scrap book. He reads every piece of mail and displays it all for a day or two before some cards need to be removed to make room for more. He really enjoys the artistic cards that come to him from various classrooms across the country and around the world. At 13 years old, he deeply appreciates the well wishes and is encouraged by the prayers that you all make for him. On his behalf I want to thank all those who sent cards and gifts for his birthday as well as for all the regular "get well" cards. They brighten up his days.

We continue to live under the grace of God and experience his blessing and presence in our lives in the midst of difficult times.

john & bonita - lorien, christopher, Julian, reuben, martin

Chapter Two

He Will Not Let Your Foot Slip

Days 27-161

Day 27

Dear Family and Friends of Julian

Today the doctors took a bone marrow sample from Julian's hip. This was to determine whether Julian's leukemia had responded to the chemotherapy by going into full remission. This indeed was the case. 27 days ago, Julian's bone marrow was approx. 99% malignant cells; today it was zero %. You can imagine that there was a "stereo" sigh of relief from Bonita and me, as Dr. Louis told us the results of today's procedure. Though we were told that the induction chemo is effective in 95% of patients there was still some tension as we awaited the results. The Lord in his grace has granted your and our requests and petitions and blessed the treatments of the last month by beating the leukemia back.

As I pointed out before, remission is defined by 100% disease free status. This is not yet a cure, however. This is but the "beach-head" from which to work. From here on, it is time to build and consolidate the "beach-head." Dr. Louis likes to point out that four weeks ago the leukemia was the boss; now he is. Though we as Christian parents, recognize that God is sovereign in this matter as he is in all others, we understand Dr. Louis's point. Great gains have been made in the past four weeks.

Dr. Louis also told us that Julian's "genetic markers" place him within the medium risk group. They give no special concerns or difficulties. The doctor's evaluation defines Julian as a medium risk patient. This does not mean that his prognosis is significantly better than if he remained in the high-risk group, rather it means that his treatment will be less aggressive; it will consist of less toxic treatments. This will allow for a better quality of life during the treatment schedule. Not using the more dangerous drugs will also mean that there also will be fewer long term side effects. Today then, we received good news, the best news we could have expected. We were prepared to proceed with a high-risk status and were pleased and thankful to God to have that downgraded to medium.

Many people want to know what Julian's prognosis is. The doctors give percentage figures of expected outcomes. Being scientists, they work with statistics. It is their way of evaluating success. But Dr. Louis also stresses that success begins to be measured not simply by outcome but also by process. Included in success is the life that is lived. Not just life after cancer - but living with cancer. The bottom line for us, who are Christ's is not, "Will Julian survive?" But can we with him live our lives to God's glory? Success is not measured simply by cheating death, but by living in Christ in all and every circumstance. Doctor Louis holds out only a 75% success rate. Small comfort for parents! Most of the 25% who succumb and die of the disease do so in the first 18 months after having one or two relapses. Our comfort is not in the 75% success rate but is given in the Heidelberg Catechism's Lord's Day 1 - especially, in this case, by the part that says, "not a hair can fall from my head...." That has special meaning, I think for patients and families living with cancer chemotherapy. Julian's hair is thinning, each strand accounted for by our Father in heaven. Julian's comfort is that he, and we then with him, belong to Christ also with our bodies; Julian belongs to Christ with his battered body.

In the coming days we hope that Julian will be able to return home for some well-deserved time off. He is really looking forward to that. Today he was "released" from protective isolation because one of his blood counts has risen past the boundary numbers. He still suffers from anemia and now also has quite severe pain from drug induced stomach ulcers, especially after eating. His diabetes is coming around, however. We hope that he will be free from insulin in the next few days. The last chemotherapy doses for his induction period are scheduled for Saturday. As this is the drug that causes the ulcers, we hope that his stomach pain will subside soon. In the meanwhile, he will likely receive day passes allowing him to leave the hospital for a few hours. Perhaps as early as tomorrow we will be able to have him home for a while.

"The Lord preserves Julian is such a way that without the will of his heavenly Father not a hair can fall from his head...."

john & bonita, lorien, christopher, Julian, reuben, martin

Day 33

Dear Family and Friends of Julian

Julian came home today! nearly five weeks after his initial diagnosis. His acute diabetes has passed and his drug induced abdominal pain has calmed down. It's an extra-special day since two of his brothers are also celebrating their (10th and 15th) birthdays today. Certainly, all cause for celebration in this family.

Because Julian had remained in hospital beyond his 28-day induction, due to the complications from his chemo, they took the opportunity to simply begin with the next stage of his treatment. That began yesterday. We look forward to developing a "new normal" as we learn about "living with cancer." Most of Julian's therapy can be given at home with weekly visits to the clinic and tri-weekly 2–3-day admissions to the hospital. This will go on for the next 36-45 months.

Julian has been in relatively good spirits and looks forward to being home. We and Julian thank you all for your hundreds of cards & letters, as well as gifts, visits and gracious words in person, by phone, and e-mail. We thank the Lord for your prayers and intercessions made on Julian's and our behalf. Rest assured your prayers and requests for strength in troubled times were heard and granted by our faithful Father. We continue to pray that the doctors' efforts will be crowned with success by our Lord, for it is he who heals all our diseases.

My updates may become less frequent at this point but I will continue to post "journal entries" now and again as time goes on.

Thank you all for your love and Christian compassion. And once again a special thanks to those young people (especially to those Julian's own age) who took the time to send a letter or a card giving Christian encouragement. Those for Julian, were the most special of all. Also, a bouquet to the schools and classrooms that sent letters (grammar assignments), cards (art class) or mailed a card signed by all.

With warm and heartfelt thanks and Christian greetings from Ottawa.

john & bonita, lorien, christopher, Julian, reuben, martin

Day 60

Dear Family and Friends of Julian

Tomorrow it will be two months since Julian was diagnosed with leukemia. After the first month of hospitalization, it was good to have him home again.

But this month did not pass without its own challenges.

The first days home were very difficult for us all. Julian did not feel well at all. He also lost the security of the 24 hour per day hospital care. Being home with all its busy-ness tired him out. He also still suffered from drug induced ulcers and had very much stomach pain and abdominal pain. This has become much better in the past weeks. His blood counts are all now in the normal range. In fact, one of the basic parts of his immune system (a white blood cell count that at one time was running at about 10% of a minimum normal) now is 10% above a maximum normal!

We are getting used to the routines of drug schedules and doctor visits. Julian goes to the Cancer Clinic every Tuesday. two out of three visits are just for the day. There he gets a general checkup and blood tests are done. Sometimes he receives only one drug by IV. Every three weeks he gets a spinal tap under a light general anesthetic.

To do a spinal tap the doctor takes out some cerebral spinal fluid (CSF) for testing and injects drugs back into the CSF to protect his central nervous system (CNS) from the spread of the disease. (If the leukemia spreads into the CSF and then to the CNS it can cause blindness, brain hemorrhages, severe headaches and paralysis.) A spinal tap (or lumbar puncture) can be compared to tapping a sugar maple for syrup. A large, long needle is pushed into the lower spine and the fluid found around the brain and spinal cord drips out under its own pressure. The drugs are injected via the same large needle.

Julian also needs to be admitted to the hospital every three weeks for a 24-hour IV treatment. The drug he receives that way is so powerful and dangerous that he then needs a 24-hour antidote. If the drug levels are not down low enough after the antidote, he needs to remain for another day. Two weeks ago, on his first return visit for this treatment, Julian stayed for four days! He stayed because the drug also made him very ill and caused a lot of stomach and abdominal pain. Next Tuesday he has to go back for another of these treatments. Julian has not yet lost all his hair though week by week it is getting thinner. It is especially these treatments that cause hair loss.

His diabetic problem has cleared but because of his nausea, diabetes and ulcers as well as the drugs he was taking he had lost a lot of weight. The catabolic (opposite of anabolic) steroids he was on caused his metabolism to burn off much of his muscle mass. This caused general weakness as well as the weight loss.

Shortly after his return home he tried to pick up a two-year-old baby and severely strained his back. The muscles in his back spasmed and within a day he was unable to walk. The physiotherapist was able to loosen the muscles with massage and heat treatments and so relieve the constant pain. It became apparent, however, that his problem was much greater than it first seemed. Soon, just walking caused his muscles to spasm. His back muscles were compensating for the lack of leg strength but were also unequal to the task of walking.

Last week we got Julian a wheelchair. This is only a temporary measure and with a good exercise program he is regaining his strength. He can walk around the house and climb stairs again (without getting down on his hands and knees as he was doing two weeks ago). If he goes out, he needs his wheelchair, though he did make it to church without it on Sunday afternoon.

Dr. Louis tells us that for the next four months or so, as new complications and discouragement arise, we will be saying, "Oh, no! not this too!" but that after a while we will see the previous problems returning and they will become more manageable. We're not sure whether that is comforting or not!

We and Julian thank you for the cards and letters that continue to arrive. Also thank you to those who sent and gave gifts, make visits and who speak gracious words in person, by phone, and e-mail. Julian also sends a special "thank-you" to those brothers and sisters from Australia who have sent mail in the past month.

We thank the Lord for all your prayers and intercessions made on Julian's and our behalf. Your supplications for strength in difficult times are heard and granted by our faithful Father. We continue to pray that the doctors' efforts will be crowned with success by our Lord, for it is he who heals all our diseases.

Bonita and I were able to get away for a week to the West Coast to attend the family festivities connected to my mother's 80th birthday. A young couple of the congregation graciously took on the challenge of caring for our family. We were able to speak to many of you face to face. Apologies to

Only When It's Dark

those whom we missed - especially our cousins, Wendell K who we missed meeting face to face, Tako K who called from Calgary while back from Africa, and John S who happened to be in Ottawa while we were away.

Till next time

john & bonita, lorien, christopher, Julian, reuben and martin

Day 90

Dear Family and Friends of Julian

It is now 90 days since Julian (our 13 year old son) was diagnosed with Acute Lymphocytic Leukemia (ALL). We have been hoping to build a "new normal." But this month too, did not pass without its own challenges.

Julian had to go to the clinic today and from there be admitted to 4-East, the oncology ward at CHEO. He has been in good spirits these past days, but today started with difficulty. He had a hard time eating breakfast knowing that before the day was out his chemo would likely bring on the nausea. His chemo treatment this week is a 24-hour push and then 24 hours of antidote.

The "side effects" of the drugs are taking their toll. Dr. Louis reminds us over and over that these problems are but a "sideshow." We were getting used to the nausea, the ulcers, the weight loss, the muscle atrophy. In the past weeks, however, we have had to cope with new hurdles. Julian was unable to walk because of muscle spasms and ended up crawling on his hands and knees. With physiotherapy, however, he has been restored to his feet.

It has become apparent now that the drug Vincristine has caused some limited neurotoxicity. He has lost some muscle function in his left hand and muscle strength in his ankles. Last week his care team decided to bring in the occupational therapist. He will likely receive leg / foot braces to wear at night to keep his toes and feet from pointing down. The neurotoxicity, or as the physiotherapist calls it, the temporary peripheral neuropathy, will pass without much problem when use of this drug is no longer necessary but we need to do what we can to maintain muscle function and range of movement in Julian's hands and feet.

Today, however, we were stunned by a new major setback. Last Friday one of our sons asked if I would check his height on my study doorpost. For the past year or so my children all step up to the door frame and get their height marked and dated. Julian figured we should check his height also. We were shocked to notice that he had lost almost 3 cm since he was on a day pass visit from CHEO in late September! When we brought this to the attention of the care team, it was confirmed by their own measurements. It had passed unnoticed since his drop in height was incremental over the past 14 weeks. It was only when they checked his present height against his height at first admission that the loss was noticed. X-rays were ordered and compared to x-rays taken at Day 14. Julian has developed quite serious osteoporosis.

The chemotherapy he receives is stripping the mineral content from his bones. Julian apparently has suffered numerous compression fractures in his vertebrae. Though his loss of bone density is reversible and should begin to rebuild as his chemotherapy tapers down in the coming years, he has already suffered permanent structural damage. As Dr. Hasper said, "He will likely not attain his genetically pre-programmed maximum height." He may have lost more than two inches from his mature height. We also do not know what the effect will have with respect to arthritis or other bone and joint illnesses in his future. We need to consult with the orthopedist tomorrow. Julian could very well need a temporary body brace to help support his spine. The initial back problems were likely related to the bone degeneration.

Julian is a very active young man who now has been told, no basketball, volleyball, tobogganing, skating, or any other sport which could send sharp jolts up his spine. I am not sure the reality of this struck him today. He takes things in stride but the news nearly broke his parents' hearts. The bad news keeps chipping away at our emotional stamina. Time and again we need to turn to the Lord. We know and believe that nothing comes by chance. No, it is as with his hand that he upholds all creatures, and Julian too, and so governs them that leaf and blade, rain and drought, health and sickness, indeed all things come to us, not by chance but by his fatherly hand. In our *Book of Praise* the rhymed version of Psalm 34:8 comes to mind:

> The righteous man may grieve;
> He many troubles may endure.
> The LORD will free him from them all;
> His help is ever sure.
> Why should he then despair?
> God keeps his bones from injury;
> Not one of them will come to harm,
> For great and good is he!
>
> Though despair knocks on our door each day,
> we do confess of the Lord,
> "How great and good is he!
> Why should we then despair?"*

john & bonita, lorien, christopher, Julian, reuben and martin

---

* *Book of Praise: Anglo-Genevan Psalter* (Winnipeg: Premier, 2013), 80.

Day 108

Dear Family and Friends of Julian

Since the day we were told that Julian had developed quite serious osteoporosis we have begun to see the human side of the hospital. I'll explain. CHEO is an excellent hospital staffed with competent and caring staff; it is a hospital of professionals. But so many people have now been brought into the action that it becomes impossible for them all to know the "big picture." At CHEO Julian sees two doctors who work as a team. One is a hematologist (blood doctor) the other an oncologist (cancer doctor). Two pharmacists participate closely in his care. Monthly, these four alternate their attention between the clinic on the 6th floor and the ward on the 4th. In the clinic we have a case manager who oversees the various aspects of Julian's clinic visits. But we also visit the occupational therapist in her clinic and the physiotherapist in hers, as well as the dentist in hers. Julian regularly visits radiology for x-rays or ultrasound scans as well as the cardiology clinic for ECGs or echocardiograms of his heart. In the oncology clinic we often meet with a resident physician who is visiting for two months from the General Hospital across the parking lot. She is an adult oncologist expanding her knowledge into pediatric cancer. We usually visit with a nurse practitioner who is qualified to assess Julian on an ongoing basis and perform the regular procedures. The hematologist has an intern working with him who also performs some procedures. An orthopedic surgeon has been called in to assess his osteoporosis. Two endocrinologists have been consulted when Julian was diabetic. The head dietitian also has been consulted.

On the ward and in the clinic, Julian benefits from the care of Child Life workers as well as a number of volunteers in the playroom. Besides all these there is a team of competent and wonderful nurses who work in the clinic as well as on the ward. (The nurses are the actual care givers!) And then there are the clinic and ward receptionists who book appointments, take information, provide information and attempt to get us all to the various people on time and in good spirits. To this we can add the anesthetists who come to the clinic when Julian's schedule demands a lumbar puncture or bone marrow aspiration, the social workers who are there to support and encourage us, and other support staff. CHEO is truly an amazing place. And now we have been sent "off campus" to an orthotist who will make and fit Julian with his body brace.

As I said, so many people have now been brought into the action that it becomes impossible for them all to know the "big picture." We are beginning to deal with the breakdown in communication between the players. They cannot all get together to discuss the plan of action. There are various views and ideas on how to proceed. The physiotherapist wants to address the osteoporosis with exercise; the orthopedist wants a brace. Mother wants to give calcium supplements. We suggested calcium supplements from the start because there was a fear of osteoporosis, but one doctor said, "No, his kidneys will not handle it." When it became apparent how bad his bones were another doctor prescribed large doses of elemental calcium and vitamin D.

The next day we got a phone call telling us not to fill the prescriptions because the first doctor said, "No!" When a new physiotherapist was assigned to Julian, I simply took the time to explain what his status was. When one of the doctors came by to discuss something I quickly realized that the two had never met before, even though they were part of the same care team! I introduced them to each other. We have decided to take a much more proactive role in Julian's care. The mystique of the hospital is slipping. We still have confidence in CHEO, but we now certainly begin to realize that we need to be advocates for Julian in the midst of a huge organization, an organization where not everyone agrees what is the best course of action.

Tomorrow Julian needs to be admitted again for his 24-hour IV push. He has gone three times. He has three more of these to go. He does not look forward to them. By this time tomorrow the anti-nausea drugs will be working full time.

We thank the Lord for all your continued encouragement and prayers. Sustained by the Lord's grace and mercy, granted by your prayers, we are able to carry on with joy and confidence, anticipating future grace from him.

Living in the hope of the coming New Jerusalem

john & bonita, lorien, christopher, Julian, reuben and martin

Day 109

Dear Family and Friends of Julian

Julian was admitted to 4-East today. This morning we left home for CHEO at about 8:30. For the first time Julian went in rather high spirits. He ate his breakfast and headed out with his knapsack full of schoolbooks ready to face the hospital one more time. What a difference 12 hours makes! After teaching catechism tonight, I dropped by the hospital. Our son was curled up in his bed with a bowl handy. His cheeks were flushed, his eyes flooding with tears. Though his mother and siblings were visiting he had no interest in what was going on around him. The IV pump was clicking quietly in the background slowly feeding the chemicals into his blood; chemicals to save his life; chemicals which momentarily rob him of joy and pleasure; chemicals to make him sick. You'd think you might get used to this - but I cannot.

On Friday Johnny died. Johnny had Down's syndrome. (For some inexplicable reason there is a connection between Down's Syndrome and ALL). Johnny relapsed this fall and the doctors were unable to get him to achieve a second remission. Johnny died while visiting the clinic on 6-North. He was 20 and should have been at an adult hospital. CHEO only takes patients up to 18. They bent the rules to keep Johnny out of the "mean" hospitals. He died while on a day visit.

Yesterday Amy died. Amy was a young girl whose cancer could not be conquered. Amy died on 4-East. There was not much joy in the Clinic or on the Ward today. The hard reality of cancer does not leave the doctors and nurses untouched. One doctor told me that it was heart rending to be there as Amy's parents said goodbye to their little girl. Her death was not unexpected but each death takes its toll. It spurs the hospital on to do better for the next child, the next family, the next parents. But each death is a defeat for these people who battle death each step of the way.

These two deaths brought to sharp relief the battle in which Julian is engaged. This is a life and death struggle. Dr. Hasper and Dr. Louis fight - No holds barred! No quarter given! His osteoporosis? On a scale of 1 to 10? Dr. Louis gives it a four! His neuropathy? Maybe a two! It is the Johnnys and Amys that face the 8's and 9's and 10's. Yet, when I held my son in my arms tonight, I wept. I wept for him and for his mother - even as I weep now as I write these words. I weep for Johnny's family, for Amy's parents, for the doctors and the nurses who loved them and cared for them. When we left CHEO tonight Julian was quietly crying. His nurse Lynn came to sit with him and comfort him and hold his hand.

The scripture teaches us: Humble yourselves, therefore, under God's mighty hand, that he may lift you up in due time. Cast all your anxiety on him because he cares for you .... because he cares for you ... because he cares for you.

Lord, have mercy.

john & bonita, lorien, christopher, Julian, reuben and martin

Day 112

Dear Family and Friends of Julian

Julian's stay at CHEO was extended for a day. Exactly 48 hours after his chemotherapy begins the IV nurse comes by to take a blood sample in order to determine the drug levels in his body. If they are still high (his treatment lasts for 24 hours followed by 24 hours of antidote) - if his drug levels are still high, he needs to remain "hooked up" to "Charlie," his IV pole. The fluids that they give him are necessary to flush the drugs back out of his body. He was not a happy camper when he heard that he was not allowed to come home and had to stay "hooked up." His anti-nausea drugs also were not as effective as during past admissions. And he is sick and tired of hospital food. Last night he asked that we "smuggle in" some Kentucky Fried Chicken. He was hungry, having sent his supper tray back. He ate his chicken with gusto - but in the end, he couldn't keep it down. He rather philosophically chewed on a bone and said, "Since you went out and got it for me, the least I can do is enjoy the taste!"

I spoke to him on the phone just now and he is feeling quite well, though he has not yet eaten today. "I'm not hungry." That means that in the last 72 hours he has managed to eat and keep down only two or three very light meals. It is a real challenge for him to keep his weight up. When he gets home today, we will need to get used to him eating six times a day again, as he makes up for lost ground. He wants to break 45 kg /100 lb.

He has taken on a new hobby. Julian has become a model builder. Andrea, the child life worker, often has a new model auto or airplane for him. Dr. Louis "badgers" Julian a bit. "What can I do for you? What can I get you?" And Julian usually answers with a shrug of the shoulders, "Nothing, really." Once he said, "You can buy me a Corvette!" We all had a good chuckle. Well, this week he got his Corvette! He just needs to glue it together yet.

Dr. Louis also badgers Julian to show more emotion about his situation. The Doctor expects his young patients to react to their diagnosis with frustration and anger. Julian, however, is very calm about it all. Recently the doctor asked Julian why he was so quiet. "Why don't you show some anger?"

Julian just shrugged his shoulders. When the doctor had left the room Julian turned to me and asked incredulously, "Who should I be mad at? God?"

Julian's foot braces don't bother him much anymore; he can wear them through the night now without pain. The occupational therapist has also made an ingenious splint for his semi-paralyzed little finger. Using the special plastics she works with she made a double ring, like a figure eight, which Julian can use to tie his little finger to his ring finger. He is measured up for his body brace, but it will not be ready for some weeks yet.

Next week and the week after he is scheduled to get the drug that causes the neuropathy and peripheral paralysis. Along with this drug, he gets the drug that is a major player in the bone demineralization and muscle loss. He's not taken these two drugs since mid-October. We wonder what the New Year will bring. We know for certain, however, that whatever happens we will continue to enjoy new mercies every morning for "great is your faithfulness, O Lord! great is your faithfulness!"

Morning by morning new mercies we see!

john & bonita, lorien, christopher, Julian, reuben and martin

New Year's Day 1997 *Day 124*

Dear Family and Friends of Julian

A new year has begun. We stand at the threshold and in a way as never before our family looks ahead with anticipation. We wonder what the Lord has in store for us. We reflect on the mercy shown to us. We strive to live humbly under the mighty hand of God, and we know that he cares for us. After four months we are developing that "new normal" that was promised us by friends who walked this road before us. It is not that we get used to the idea of cancer, but rather that by the grace of God, we are learning to cope with the demands, the routines and the fragility of our lives. We are learning over and over that God's grace is sufficient; God abounds in grace for each new day.

Julian has come into contact with two boys who broke out with chicken pox two days later. They were visitors to our congregation and mingled among the children after the young people of the congregation put on a Christmas program. Chicken pox is a scourge for childhood cancer patients. Julian has had this illness and so likely has enough antibodies to protect him, but a related illness, shingles, might break out. He needs to be admitted to CHEO next week for his regular chemo. He will be held in strict isolation, segregated from all other patients on the ward (to protect them from a potential outbreak). That means no Playroom activities, no walks in the halls, no roommate.

Julian was in high spirits last week. The catabolic steroids he was on caused him to be energetic and gregarious. It was great! He was bounding with energy. We had not seen him like this for months. His indomitable spirit shone through day after day. His jokes and puns were a cause for laughter for all.

john & bonita, lorien, christopher, Julian, reuben and martin

Day 147

Dear Family and Friends of Julian

Julian did not get chicken-pox. For this we are very thankful. A bout of chickenpox would have meant a 10 day stay at CHEO. He has only one more scheduled three day stay at CHEO! In mid-February his program moves on and he will be taking almost all his chemotherapy drugs orally. This will be a significant change. As the chemotherapy program becomes less intense, we also become more aware of the possibility of relapse. We place our hope and trust in the Lord that all will be well. We place our confidence in him, that he will avert all evil or change it to our good.

On Tuesday, at the clinic, Julian was asked if he could go to the Corel Center (the local NHL hockey arena) to attend a

Press Conference and officially open a Box Suite (of 12 seats) that Wade Redden a rookie Senators defenseman had purchased and donated to CHEO to be used by sick children and their families. Julian gladly did this, for which he made it on CBC, CTV and TSN news and sports casts. Even Julian's oldest brother, Shaun (who lives in Alberta) saw his little brother on TV. He called yesterday and said that while he was watching TSN he thought, "That looks like my little brother! Hey! That *is* my little brother!" Julian also graced the front pages of the Ottawa Citizen and the Ottawa Sun. Throughout the whole city his smiling face looked out from every news-stand and paper box. He received 7 tickets for himself and his family to go the Hockey Game and enjoy the new suite. This we did last night. A good time was had by all, even though the Senators lost 4 to 1 to Boston!

john & bonita, lorien, christopher, Julian, reuben and martin

Day 161

Dear Family and Friends of Julian

Last week Julian returned to CHEO for his last scheduled in-patient chemotherapy. This is a milestone on the way. The drug protocol had given him two weeks off beforehand. It was as if his body had acclimatized to the low levels of drugs in his body because he became violently ill from the treatments. Upon admission Julian has the IV apparatus connected to his permanent chest catheter. When they administer the drugs, they begin with a large syringe full. In merely moments (90 seconds or so) Julian can taste the drug! His saliva immediately becomes bitter. He usually tries to eat something or chew gum while the first of the drugs are pushed into his veins. By Tuesday evening he was feeling poorly. On Wednesday the nausea got out of control. The nausea is controlled using a new generation of drugs which work on the neuro - transmitters in the brain. These drugs actually suppress the nausea center in the brain. However, if the nausea actually "breaks through" it becomes very difficult to control. This happened on Wednesday evening. In their attempt to control vomiting and gagging the doctors order up six different anti-nausea drugs were administered to our son. The Gravol and Benadryl also cause drowsiness. This pushed Julian into a semi - conscious state but sleep would not come. As the hours went by, he became more and more desperate for sleep. In tears and a sort of delirium he cried for sleep but the nausea and vomiting kept him awake into the night. Finally, the nurses were able to give him another drug that calmed him down and the Lord gave him blessed sleep. He did manage to sleep through the night. We are thankful that this was the sixth of six such treatments. It did not get easier as time went on. From Tuesday lunch (a light lunch) to Friday supper time he managed to keep down one small cookie. He has learned that it is better simply to be hungry for a few days.

When his scheduled discharge arrived, his blood drug levels were much too high so he had to stay an extra day hooked up to his IV pole. The IV fluids along with an antidote flush the chemotherapy out of his body and so "rescue" him. On the other occasions, as he recovered from this treatment, he was back in fairly good form by Friday but this time the nausea continued into Sunday. We are thankful to the Lord for the anti-nausea drugs that make life bearable for our son. Before the advent of these powerful neurotransmitter drugs, some parents would choose not to go on with the treatment program, and instead allow their children to succumb to their disease. The chemotherapy is that unbearable! Now because of these drugs they are tolerable (barely!).

We now head into the next phase of Julian's treatments. In two weeks, he will have a bone marrow sample taken and an assessment done. We trust that he will still be in remission. Many people have asked us what the future holds. "How is Julian responding to the treatments?" they ask. Or, "Is he getting better?" Leukemia is a cancerous disease of the bone marrow. The bone marrow manufactures the various blood components. To answer these questions and to understand remission, consider the following.

A drop of blood contains 150,000,000 red blood cells. They have a life span of about 3-4 months. In other words, 1% of the total dies each day. The bone marrow, therefore, needs to produce 3,000,000 red blood cells per second (!) to keep up with the natural loss.

That same drop of blood contains 7-10,000,000 platelets. Their life expectancy is about one or two weeks unless called on to control bleeding. That means that about 10% die each day. The bone marrow needs to produce about 1,500,000 platelets per second.

That drop of blood also contains some 500,000-700,000 white blood cells of various kinds. They die off at various rates but on average the marrow makes about 250,000 per second.

This all means that the bone marrow of a healthy adolescent or adult manufactures a staggering 400 billion (!) cells per day (!). In crisis (injury or infection) this can be stepped up four or five-fold to two trillion per day.

When we examine these numbers and realize that these cells are created by cloning (cell division) and differentiation (cell maturation) it is surprising that the fine balance of supply and demand is not disturbed more often or, as in the case with leukemia, that an error creeps into the cloning process.

Remission is defined as the fading of all signs of the disease. But remission is not a cure. Medical experts estimate that a four-year-old child will have a thousand billion (10^{12}) leukemic cells at diagnosis. This would, if lumped together, be the volume of a honeydew melon. chemotherapy might quickly reduce that to 1/1000 the volume, a very small lump. Yet it would still be one billion leukemic cells. Now scatter those billion cancerous cells throughout the body. They become invisible, undetectable and do not interfere with the normal body processes, nor do they affect normal bone marrow function. Yet there are a billion cancerous cells reproducing themselves ready to take over the blood factory once again. Remission means that there is no detectable level of cancerous cells. But that detectable level is not that low!

Reflecting on this it becomes clearer why a 2–3-year program of chemotherapy is needed to defeat this illness even though there is simply no detectable cancer in our son's body. If any of those remaining cells are drug resistant, then the possibility of relapse is high. But the relapsed leukemia then inherits the drug resistant characteristics. For this reason, the chemo program is so intense to begin with. Using 8 drugs it is hoped that no leukemic cell will survive the treatments.

We are now entering the phase in which the treatments are less aggressive. But this is also the time in which relapse is possible. 30-40% of the children will relapse, many of them (as they say) "under treatment" from 6-18 months. Relapse would mean that we would begin again at Day 1 of the program. We pray to God that this will not happen to our son. For most who relapse "under treatment," it is kind of like the first page of the last chapter.

So, "How is Julian doing?" He is in remission. His bone marrow is merrily making 400,000,000,000 cells per day. But in the midst of that might be any number of millions of cancerous cells – undetected. Any one of them is a threat to his life. We will continue to faithfully administer the terrible drugs trusting that the Lord God will bless those treatments and preserve this young man's life.

Julian is also a determined young man. Even though he did not feel 100% he went swimming on Saturday and we allowed him to go skating on the Rideau Canal on Monday.

Though he needs to take care of his back because of his osteoporosis, we saw that the ice was in good shape (and well ... you can't deny him everything!)

His body brace arrived last week. It is a one-piece molded plastic corset that tightens with two straps across his back. It was custom fitted for him and so fits him perfectly. He does not really like to, but he is beginning to wear it a few hours most days. It will help his posture and will help protect his spine from any more compression fractures.

As our family enters this next phase we do so with some uncertainty. The prospect of relapse is real. Yet we also go forward with great certainty. The Lord has our times in his hand. With him is constant faithfulness and abiding love.

john & bonita, lorien, christopher, Julian, reuben and martin

Chapter Three

The Lord Will Keep You
Days 240-910

Day 240

Dear Family and Friends

It has been quite some time that you have heard from us. Many have asked how Julian is doing. Julian is doing quite well. That first of all, his weekly visits have become routine. Every Tuesday we go to CHEO. After Julian's last admission to the hospital 80 days ago he has been healthy and strong. His drug program is much different now. He has to take a much lower dosage of the drugs he received while in the hospital and no longer takes them by IV but instead takes them orally. Every two weeks he takes Methotrexate (MTX), four doses exactly six hours apart. Then 48 hours later we have to rescue - that is what the doctors call it - we have to rescue him with the antidote. This drug does make him ill but not nearly as severely as it did in the hospital. With some experimentation we have found the balance between nausea and grogginess. At first Julian did not want too high a dose of the anti-nausea drug because it made him so listless, but then the nausea would win out. Now he prefers the sleepiness. We walk a fine line every two weeks. Four days out of 14 he feels less than 100%. It is quite a grueling regimen for the young man. He asked me yesterday if he had to take the MTX next week. I said, "I guess so, you're not taking it this week." He replied, "It seems as if I just quit taking it... Well, I guess I did just quit taking it!"

Last Tuesday we went to a clinic in the General Hospital where, using X-rays, they are able to determine Julian's bone density. We are hoping that his bones, which have been stripped of much of their calcium, might be recovering. The results of this test will determine much of Julian's quality of life for the next while. Summer-time activities will be curtailed if his bones remain as fragile as they were in the late fall. He hates wearing his body brace.

Julian continues to visit the physiotherapist. He is working on strengthening his back and keeping his legs limber. We noticed some months ago that Julian had no reflexes in his arms and legs. One of the doctors did just about everything to get a knee jerk and was not successful. The drug Vincristine apparently had done more damage than at first thought. His paralysis in his hand has cleared but this seemed to be permanent. Two weeks ago, Dr. Hughs suggested that perhaps over the next 5-7 years there might be some restoration. Last week, however, his reflexes suddenly were restored to a quite remarkable strength. So much of what is going on is as much a mystery to the doctors as it is to us. The drugs work. How? Not everything is clear. The side effects are different for every patient. Much is very unpredictable. We are fearfully and wonderfully made!

As summer comes, we are also aware of the sun's strength. The MTX that Julian takes may not be exposed to sunshine. The pills must be kept from sunlight because the drug's chemistry changes under UV rays. It is photo sensitive. Since Julian has quite high levels of MTX in his body we must keep him out of the sun. He has become photo sensitive! If he would receive high levels of UV light, the drug will cause 2nd degree burns to his skin – from the inside out! Long sleeves, long pants, floppy hats and #45 sun-block are the order of the day. We are already adjusting his (home) school schedule to allow him to be outside before 10 and after 3 when the sun's rays are not as strong.

Two months ago, Julian's second to last bone marrow sample was taken. Unless relapse is suspected he will not need that procedure till the very end. The last will be taken at Day 910. (We are more than 25% to that goal.) Julian has not missed any chemo because of illness or liver problems. He has only had one bout with a fever and is gaining height and weight.

John van Popta

We hope and pray that the Lord will grant him the health and strength to press on to the end.

We continue to be encouraged by the love and compassion shown by so many of God's people. We truly have been sustained by your prayers and continue to live day by day, confessing that God's grace is sufficient for us. Thanks be to God for the love he shows to us via the hearts and hands of his saints.

john & bonita, lorien, christopher, Julian, reuben and martin

Day 286

Dear Family and Friends

Julian continues to make good progress. The leukemia is still in remission. The chemotherapy program continues unabated. Julian has not missed any treatments or doses due to complications. His liver is successfully metabolizing the chemo. He has not developed ulcers, mouth sores, shingles, pneumonia or any of the other common side effects related to his program. His hair, once quite thin, is thick and blond as can be. His blood counts continue to be within the acceptable range. Though they are quite low compared to "normal" children, he has shown remarkable physical stamina.

Some time ago Julian had a bone density scan. You might

remember that he had developed serious osteoporosis as a side effect of his drug therapy combined with the nature of his illness. Last October Julian was unable to walk and ended up in a wheelchair because of multiple compression fractures in his spine. The bone scan now shows that the bones are re-mineralizing and have gone from 40% to 80% of normal in his lower back and to 40% to 62% in his upper spine and neck. This progress is cause for thankfulness as the likelihood of more fractures begins to fade. He must still avoid all high impact sports (all court sports, as well as running).

Even as progress is made in one area, new areas of concern open up. The treatment program that Julian is on is the result of 20 or more years of research. The drug protocol undergoes constant evolution and evaluation. The protocol he is following was initiated in April of 1996, four months before his diagnosis. This schedule is the first that uses absolutely no radiation therapy. Instead, the drug doses are much higher. It seems, however, that for some of the children these high drug doses are neuro-toxic. Julian had troubles with paralysis in his hands and feet and has lost most of his reflex function in his limbs. For many children, however, there is increasing evidence that the drugs are affecting brain function and development, especially in math and problem-solving skills. All the patients on the program in North America are undergoing neuro-psychological testing in which the doctors are attempting to isolate those children who are at risk. They also may be able to identify the neurotoxicity with MRI scans of the brain. Julian has undergone the first 6 hours of testing and had an MRI scan. He still needs another 3-4 hours of testing. We do not think that Julian shows any signs of these problems but he is an interesting patient for he is among the older group in whom extensive testing can be done. He is an intriguing specimen! We certainly hope and pray that not many patients will need to go back to radiation therapy. The radiation is concentrated on the central nervous system (CNS) (brain, brainstem, spinal cord) as preventative measure. It makes the children very ill, and inevitably, completely bald.

Julian had a spinal tap and CNS treatment yesterday. He now gets that treatment every two months. He also is on his regular bi-weekly treatments as well as the drug that causes nerve paralysis. This drug is boosted by the steroids that cause the osteoporosis. Considering that he was on 10 different drugs yesterday, and today he is doing remarkably well. He is gaining weight and height.

Last week we read in the Ottawa Citizen (our local paper) about how the Children's Hospital in Vancouver made a tragic error with a seven-year-old patient who was undergoing the same treatment as Julian is. They got her drugs mixed up and injected the drug (Vincristine) that causes the nerve paralysis directly into her spine instead of intravenously. She died within the hour. Needless to say, we were rather taken aback. Vancouver Children's Hospital is one of the leading hospitals in the country. We did ask at CHEO what procedures they take to avoid such a terrible accident from happening. We cannot imagine the horror that the doctor and staff must need to endure, much less imagine the sorrow and anger of the parents of that little girl.

Two weeks from now Julian will have completed 1/3 of his treatment schedule without missing a day because of illness or complications. For this we thank the Lord who is the Great Physician, the one who heals all our diseases. We acknowledge also that we are sustained daily by the Lord who answers the prayers of his people, and we thank him for the love shown by so many, so faithfully, over so many weeks and months.

God's grace is sufficient for us.

john & bonita, lorien, christopher, Julian, reuben and martin

Day 365

Dear family and friends of Julian

This coming Saturday it will be a year ago that our son Julian was diagnosed with ALL. Julian and I discussed what we were going to do to celebrate his "anniversary." He wants to take the family bowling! He is in good health and spirits.

One year! In certain ways it seems ages ago that we visited Julian in the hospital every day. We have learned many things about hospitals, drugs, treatments, side-effects. We have come to know many gracious and kind and thoughtful people. Julian moves with confidence through the corridors and rooms of CHEO (the hospital) and MDU (the Medical Day Unit). Many people in the hospital have come to know him and his cheerful smile.

You all know that Julian must visit the MDU once per week. Every Tuesday morning Julian and I head out to CHEO. We wanted to go on vacation, to a cottage provided by dear friends for three weeks but Julian had his clinic appointments. So we arranged that he would have his blood work done on Monday morning early, in the lab. We then could head out on vacation. The following Monday we were to visit a hospital close to the cottage with a requisition for blood work. That allowed us two weeks away. The 3rd week we had to head back for a Tuesday visit. 15 days was the most that they would allow us. We had to travel back 560 km (350 miles) - one way - to see his doctors. We did have a wonderful vacation.

Julian managed to do some wilderness hiking. We took backpacks, sleeping bags and tents, and headed up the Bruce Trail from Emmet Lake to Tobermory. (Ontario people will know where that is.) This is very rugged country along the limestone cliffs of the Niagara Escarpment and along the rocky shores of the Georgian Bay. Julian carried a light back and managed to walk the 28 km (18 miles) over the two days. It was good for him and for us to see that he was strong enough to keep up with his dad and older brother and sister.

Since returning home from vacation he has developed a cough. It seems as if the feared pneumonia is invading his lungs. He has some fluid in his left lung but with an extra antibiotic the doctors hope to keep it under control and knock it back. He has not developed a fever, which is reason for optimism that this is but a minor difficulty. We are reminded, however, how fragile he really is. His immune system is still severely compromised, and the threat of pneumonia or infection is constant.

Julian no longer wears his back brace. He suffers from no paralysis (though his reflexes in his legs and arms are barely there.) His bones have remineralized. He does suffer from bouts of nausea but on the whole eats and drinks like any other 13-year-old. Many children become ill and are unable to press on with their treatment schedule. Julian, however, made it to "Week 52" at his "anniversary." He has not missed a single treatment. For this we are very thankful.

On another note - Many of you may have heard of the "Children's Wish Foundation." The CWF grants the wishes of terminally ill children. Many children go to Disney Land or Disney World with their families or go to visit some famous actor or athlete. There are other foundations that also grant wishes to sick children. The Starlight Foundation is one of them. Their criterion for granting wishes is not that the child must be suffering a terminal illness but simply a life-threatening illness. Julian was informed that he could have a wish granted by the Starlight Foundation. It did not take him long to wish for a computer. He was told that he could consider taking his family to Disney World or something like that but he countered, "Disney World is just for a few days and then it's gone. A computer is for life!" For life! He radiates optimism. He does not think of his illness as life-threatening – just a bother. He also said that he could share his computer with his brothers. They have enjoyed it for many hours this past month.

Then a few weeks ago, Robert, the child life worker asked Julian if he would like to go to Disney World, anyway! The Sunshine Foundation is organizing a one-day trip to Disney for children from CHEO. 80 children and 40 volunteers will head out early one morning on a chartered plane. They will fly from Ottawa to Orlando. There busses and more volunteers will take the children for a VIP Day at Disney World. After 8 hours of fun, the plane will return them for a late-night reunion with their families in Ottawa. With a smile, Julian quipped, "I'm glad I wished for a computer! I get to go to Disney World, after all!"

Next week Julian's drug protocol will change again. The dosages of the MTX will drop again (that's the drug that makes him so ill) but he will be getting it every week via an intermuscular needle (IM). Initially it was administered every three weeks by IV, then every two weeks orally, now every week IM. The doctors assure us that most patients don't suffer nausea from the IM treatments.

As parents, however, we are painfully aware that the drug doses are being lowered again. We hope and pray that the

Lord has blessed the treatments with good success and that the drugs are not just holding the leukemia at bay. We know that for some, as the doses are lowered, the illness comes back full force. We trust that the Lord will provide us with all things necessary and that he will continue to hold Julian, as if in his hand.

john & bonita, lorien, christopher, Julian, reuben and martin

Day 434

Dear family and friends of Julian

Connor died. Connor was a roommate of Julian in one of his "hospital weeks" last year. Once again, we are confronted with the terrible and harsh reality of cancer in children. Connor was 7. It doesn't seem right that these children should die from such terrible diseases. As we meet more people, we are confronted with death more often. There is an unreal side to this, though. The children who are doing well come to the day clinic on 6-North. Schedules change, programs proceed and the parents and children we meet there are constantly changing. Those who are going "off treatment" come less often and eventually quit coming all-together. But then there are those who quit coming to the clinic because they have been admitted to 4-East again. The other parents don't always know if a child has gone "off treatment" because of good results, or if that child isn't at the clinic anymore because of complications, relapse or death. It is always a shock when death comes. Often death comes swiftly. It's like a slap in the face. Connor died. Death is a reality with which we all must deal, but it is one which families living with cancer face in a very real way.

We recently have heard of acquaintances whose son has also been diagnosed with ALL. Tyler is the seventh and youngest child in their family. Tyler is eight years old. He was diagnosed with this serious and deadly illness in the past weeks. The doctors started chemotherapy immediately and Tyler and his family are now enduring what we endured some 60 weeks ago. Let us all commend Tyler and his family to the mercy of God. Tyler has had some complications with his blood's clotting ability. His platelet count is very low and he is having bad reactions to transfusions. The doctors do not yet understand what is happening. Let us hope and pray that these difficulties can be understood and treated.

I will never forget the joy that mail brought to Julian as he underwent days and weeks of chemotherapy. I will never forget the joy it brought to Bonita and me. Drop Tyler a card in the mail. Send him a note. Encourage his parents. Pray for them that they will continue to trust in the Lord in the days and weeks and months ahead. Support his brothers and sisters. The effect of childhood cancer on families is life changing and can be shattering. Each member of the family is confronted by it in different ways. And remember if you meet Tyler's siblings or parents, don't just ask them how Tyler is doing, ask also how they themselves are doing!

Julian is doing well. He is healthy, strong and growing like a weed. It is almost as if the first year of chemo kept him compressed like a coil spring. Now that the doses are much lighter, he is just sprouting up and out. He's gained 7 kgs since August! Dr. Hughs, who had not seen him for a few months commented today in wonderment at his stature. When he checked his reflexes, Julian's leg jerked out in good and proper fashion. You might remember that his reflexes had been suppressed and masked by the drugs. The doctors had suggested that perhaps 5-7 years might show some improvement. One year later things are returning to normal!

At the turning of the "year" Julian's treatment schedule changed again. He no longer gets such high dosages of the chemo. (It is amazing that every time I type "chemo" it inadvertently comes out "Chemo." I guess that says something about how these terrible drugs are viewed in our lives! They get respect! But yet, the big C is not chemo or cancer but Christ! Julian is now in what is called "maintenance." Pills every night. A weekly shot in his thigh. The next day is a bit of a low day. There is no nausea, though; a year of that is more than any child should have to bear. Every two months a spinal treatment and some other drugs. Most of it is bearable. For this we thank the Lord.

Week 65 will mark the mid-point of his treatment schedule! We are nearly halfway! But yet there is no halfway for cancer patients. Under the blessing of the Lord, Julian will need to go for yearly check-ups and evaluations throughout his life.

As parents we need to fight against becoming "drug dependent." It is rather frightening to have the treatment schedule become lighter; it is as if we depend on the chemo for Julian's progress and the defeat of his cancer. Doctors offer hopes for cures; Jesus Christ heals. We know and confess that it is Lord Jesus who blesses these treatments. "Cast all your anxiety on him, for he cares for Julian."

Julian now is able to do most of what any other 14-year-old can do. He is growing stronger by the day. We hope and pray that the Lord will continue to bless his treatments with good results.

Under the Mercy

john & bonita, lorien, christopher, Julian, reuben and martin

Christmas Day 1997 *Day 482*

Dear Family and friends

Julian is in the hospital again. That's not anyone's favorite place to be on Christmas Day. On Monday he began developing a rash on his back. At the clinic they thought nothing of it. By Tuesday the rash had appeared under his arm and above his heart. He complained of sharp, deep pain. Shingles! Last year he suffered from osteoporosis (some call that an "old woman's disease"). Now he has shingles (an "old man's disease")!

Shingles is a disease associated with the chicken pox virus. When patients who have had chicken pox in the past also have a suppressed immune system (seniors and chemo patients, and especially children with leukemia) this virus can become active again. When it reappears, however, it appears in the nervous system. The virus produces a rash along a nerve tract. This rash can be very painful because the viral infection is actually in the nervous system. It sometimes becomes necessary to manage the pain with morphine; so far, our boy has been spared that.

This is why Julian has been admitted to CHEO. Shingles is a scourge for childhood cancer patients. The zoster virus associated with chickenpox and shingles can infiltrate the central nervous system and cause severe damage. There are effective and powerful anti-viral drugs that can be used but they must be administered intravenously. We pray the Lord bless these medicines to good effect. He may not be admitted to the oncology (cancer) ward because of the risk of infection for other patients. Julian is, therefore, in another ward different from previous admissions. Even now he is in strict isolation in his room. He may not leave the room at all.

Julian suffers from low grade nausea all the time because of his chemo. It does not usually affect his daily life. If there are changes in his routine, new stresses or pressures, new drugs, it usually means that the nausea "breaks through" which then wracks his body for hours on end. Thus, it was yesterday morning. There seemed to be no end to it. Today was better.

We managed to get him a pass and "break him out of solitary" so that he could join us for dinner tonight. He came home at around 6:00 PM but must return to CHEO by 11:00 to be hooked up to "Charlie" his IV pole. He has no appetite (not even for Christmas dinner) though he did join us at table. His uncle and aunt and cousins are visiting and so it was a joy for us all to have him at home, even if only for a few hours. He enjoys just lying about, close to the action, though he is very quiet and subdued. His usual cheerful nature banished.

For the first time since his diagnosis nearly 500 days ago, Julian is missing his daily chemo doses. For many patients 100 days would have been missed by now because of complications. We thank the Lord for answering our prayers that he makes this hard road less difficult to travel. We pray that this be only a minor setback. We entrust our son to the care of his Father; we lay our children in his hands. May God be merciful and bless us. May he be good to Julian.

Under the mercy; at the foot of the cross

john & bonita, lorien, christopher, Julian, reuben, martin

Day 487

Dear Family and friends

Julian is home again. We were able "to break him out of solitary" on Sunday afternoon. He is feeling much better, though his rash still causes discomfort during the day and pain in the night. We are thankful for powerful anti-viral drugs that were able to bring this problem under control. Julian's outbreak of shingles has put his chemo program on hold. That means that for the past week he has not taken any chemo at all. This is not a pleasant development for us. Though we know that Julian's health and welfare is in the hand of our Father in heaven, yet we as Reformed confessors believe that God uses "means" such as chemotherapy to restore health. Julian has not missed a single week of his protocol until now. His program will now be one or two weeks longer. Nothing is missed.

He is enjoying the break, though. After 16 months of relentless daily chemotherapy a few days off seem like a holiday for him! Things should be on track again in a week or so.

We continue to trust that the Lord will support us through each new day.

john & bonita, lorien, christopher, Julian, reuben, martin

Day 710

Dear Family and friends

It has been 101 weeks since Julian was diagnosed with ALL. It has been months since my latest update. Our son has been blessed with good health these past months. Since his attack of shingles last winter, he has had no other serious complications other than a touch of pneumonia which only slowed him down for a week or so. The Lord has answered your many prayers with a "Yes!" for Julian. The doctors are pleased with his progress. Many of the children miss weeks and months of their program because of illness, infection and complications. Julian is not even one week behind schedule. His week-long episode of Shingles at Christmas was not considered as a serious disruption of his drug protocol. He will, the Lord willing, go off treatment in February 1999 exactly 130 weeks from diagnosis. 30 years ago, virtually all children diagnosed with ALL died within a year; a few exceptions survived beyond treatment. Now 65-80% make it through their treatment programs and go on to live happy and healthy lives.

I spoke to the parents of one of the other patients (a Down syndrome girl). She will be off treatment in two weeks. They have come to the closing page of their treatment book. Mom said that going off treatment is scary, in a way. We agreed that the parents all become drug dependent. Even as Christians, who rely on the Lord, it is not difficult to have hope sustained by drugs and doctors. We need to constantly be turned to the Lord who makes medical advances possible. It is he who blesses treatment programs with "Yes" and success, or answers prayers with "No, my child, it must be different from what you desire." One of the little girls who was on the ward with Julian when he was first diagnosed is losing her fight. Each day is a battle for her. Her name is Julia. I spoke to her parents today. They were in ICU with their daughter. She was struggling for each breath; her lungs are damaged from too many bouts of pneumonia and from damage caused by inhaling vomit during surgery. Julia has had two bone marrow transplants: the first failed. Julia is weak. Julian, on the other hand is strong, healthy and full of energy and life. Julia's parents are also Christians. They too pray for their little girl. The ways of the Lord are inscrutable.

In the past month there were indications that the Lord might direct our lives to a new city, a new congregation. I needed to tell my children of possibilities, of uncertainties. When Julian heard that perhaps a call to another congregation would come, he was stunned. "Where would I go to the hospital? How would I get to CHEO?" Three weeks ago, I gently told him that there were other hospitals, other doctors, other nurses as good as those he knew. For the first time since his diagnosis, we saw him weep. He just put his head on the table and wept. At times in the last year and a half tear filled his eyes. There were times when he felt so awful that he cried softly, quietly. But not now. Now he wept.

Looking at my son I realized how much we love that place, he and I, how much we love those people, the doctors, the nurses. I realized how much security we find in the midst of those who care for our son. How much security and comfort there is among those who understand. I realized how little those who don't know cancer can really understand. In that moment I learned that hope lies in covenant. Hope comes from God through people. Hope is real in relationships. It is as if Julian has made a pact with CHEO; his doctors with him. Till death do us part! There is hope in that statement. Marriage starts with that. Faithful! Till death do us part! So also, cancer kids and those who hope to cure them.

We are moving to Alberta. Many of you know that I have

received and accepted a call to Coaldale. Last week and again today we needed to say "Good-bye" to many of our friends at CHEO. I find it very difficult to part ways with the doctors, nurses and care givers whom the Lord has used to bring our son back from death's door. We have come to know and love the many people who dedicate their lives to caring for the little ones. We have only one more visit here at CHEO in Ottawa and then the next will be in Calgary at Alberta Children's Hospital. They tell us that the care there is as good as here (we can hardly believe that!) There were tears (mine) as we parted ways with these wonderful people. Julian takes it pretty much in stride. I think deep inside, though, he is bothered by our move. He doesn't speak much about it. But when we first told our children that we might be moving to Alberta, the first thing he asked was, "Where will I go to the hospital?"

We indicated that there were other places where he could get good care. He just put his head down on the table and wept. It was the first time he cried about anything related to his illness (other than during the drug induced nausea of the early treatments).

He has never complained or muttered or cried about anything. Moving, however, was too much to bear. Yet now for him it has become just one more part of his life's experience.

I asked him once on the way to the hospital what he thought of all this? "About what?" he asked. I replied, "Being ill? and the chemo? and all that was related to it, the nausea, the complications and the troubles?" He answered, "Oh! It's OK, Dad. This is my life. And it is OK." We all need to learn that simple faith: "This is my life, and under God's grace, it is OK."

john & bonita, lorien, christopher, Julian, reuben and martin

Day 850

Dear Friends and Family

We are thankful to the Lord for and with Julian (our now 15 year old son). Julian continues to receive chemotherapy for leukemia (ALL) He is doing remarkably well. At the hospital yesterday the nurses were all excited because he is now 5ft 10 and growing like a weed. Julian has finished 28 months of treatment; he has two months to go! February 25 is his scheduled "going off treatment celebration!" You can imagine that 28 months ago that seemed like a distant goal with death a more real prospect. He is now healthy, strong, exuberant, mischievous and enjoying life! He plays hockey on Mondays and lives a pretty normal life. We do not know (none of us do, of course), we do not know what the Lord has in store for us, but with childhood cancer this unknown persists. "Going off treatment" will be, in itself, a new worry. As parents and patient, we realize that many children will relapse in the weeks and months after treatment stops. What is in store for Julian? Please continue to pray that the Lord will care for him in the coming weeks and months. And remember that the Lord has already answered your many prayers with a "Yes!"

Now that we live in southern Alberta, instead of Ottawa, we make the trip to the Children's hospital in Calgary once every three or four weeks. That takes all day. We leave here at 6:15 AM for 9:00 AM appointments. Usually wait around for lab results and visit other clinics (ultra-sound, heart specialist, bone density, endocrinology, MRI, dentist, etc.) Some of these clinics are at Foothills hospital across the Bow River, a 10-minute drive away. We do make it back home by suppertime. Last Thursday we were caught in inclement winter weather on the way home. There were white-out warnings and road closures all over Alberta. We made it home without incident, however. On the other weeks (for Julian still gets weekly chemo) we go to the Cancer Clinic at Lethbridge Regional Hospital, a twenty-minute drive from our home. Julian then only misses one morning per week and one day per month of school.

When we first began our visits to Calgary the doctors were amazed to see this healthy robust teen. Because of his medical history of having all kinds of serious problems with his chemo the doctors expected to see a sickly, weakened, disease ravaged child. Instead, their patient was this strong, healthy, cheerful, "normal" teen. As we walked this road for over two years we simply accepted as normal the side effects as they came upon us. In retrospect we realize that Julian is one of the few patients who endured and survived just about every imaginable problem.

I just scanned the mail (I saved all the mail you sent us - hundreds of notes of encouragement over the past two years) and realized again how we were carried by your prayers before the throne of grace. Julian is surely evidence of the power of intercessory prayer!

With Christian and Christmas Greetings from the Canadian Prairie

John, Bonita, (Shaun, Juanita), Lorien, Christopher, Julian, Reuben, Martin

Day 910

Dear friends of Julian

Two and a half years ago, 130 weeks, or 910 days ago (August 1996) Julian was diagnosed with ALL. Many of you heard the news swiftly through family and friends. Many of you became friends through the REFNET, and because of your care and prayers for Julian. Today, Julian's treatment program comes to an end. Over the months and years our son has experienced setbacks, complications, illness, pain. Yet throughout it all we have learned to depend on the Lord who guides us day by day.

Two and a half years ago, Julian was a frightened 12-year-old; now he is a healthy, robust 15-year-old! We feared for his life that Autumn. We saw him endure the powerful drugs.

He became diabetic, contracted pneumonia (twice), was subjected to paralysis in his hands and feet (he still has very poor reflexes), had osteoporosis and multiple compression fractures in his spine. He was unable to walk (learned to use a wheelchair), wore a body brace, had stomach and intestinal ulcers, has liver cysts, drugs which threatened his heart, shingles, diabetes, compression fractures, pneumonia, all sorts of troubles, but like he says, "I never lost my hair!" He also never lost his sense of humor.

There were miserable days of pain and nausea. Sleepless nights for mom and dad. Hours and hours of waiting rooms and clinics. More doctors and specialists that I will ever remember. More miles paced in hospital corridors than should be willed on anybody. More cups of bad coffee than I care to remember.

Some weeks ago, I was reading the Globe and Mail as I was waiting in a clinic in the Alberta Children's Hospital. In the Globe and Mail there is a column called "Lives Lived." Here you can read short biographies of non-famous Canadians who recently have died. A picture of a teenage girl caught my eye. Her name jumped off the page. Six months ago, I knew her as a charming, witty young girl in Ottawa, a patient at CHEO's Cancer Clinic. She had been doing so well in her battle with bone cancer. Her mother's friend wrote her story. It ended in death by cancer. But her faith in Jesus never failed.

Yesterday, I led the funeral services for a 51-year-old parishioner, Mary. Last Tuesday the doctors told Mary that they could do no more in her battle with leukemia (AML). Mary fought this fight for three and half years. Twice chemo failed. Twice bone marrow transplants failed. Because of her illness she became completely blind. Her bones hurt. Her body was sapped of strength. On Wednesday she told me, as I came to encourage her, "God has been good to me. He has been so good to me." On Friday she could not get out of bed. On Saturday we said, "Good-bye! Until we meet again." On Sunday she went to her Lord. Every visitor who came to Mary, left encouraged. Though blind, she did not stumble in the dark. Though ill, she was not weak. Her faith never failed. "God has been so good to me."

Going off treatment! 30 months ago, we could not imagine this day. The treatment program, all 18 pages, seemed to be an insurmountable obstacle. A hill too high to climb. A valley too deep to cross. And yet here we are, on the other side. Julian plays ice hockey. He just signed up on the community soccer league today.

We do however feel as if we are stepping into a void. There is new uncertainty. New fears. Will he relapse? Is he cured, or do the drugs only hold the illness at bay? What happens next? Yet, whatever happens we can say, "The Lord has been good to us. He has been so good to us."

john & bonita, lorien, christopher, Julian, reuben and martin

CHAPTER FOUR

In the Shadow of Death
Day 1021-PSCT Day 39

Day 1021

Dear Family and friends

Just 100 days ago we were celebrating that our 15-year-old son was "going off treatment." He had endured 30 months of chemotherapy for Acute Lymphocytic Leukemia. We prayed and hoped and prayed that the treatments had the desired effect. But the Lord has decided differently. He answered our prayers for Julian with, "No, my child. No, my child, No. Julian, you will need to walk this road for some time yet."

Your journey through the valley of the shadow death is not yet over!"

During a routine exam last Tuesday, the doctors had some

concerns about Julian's health. They did some more tests. On Wednesday we were called and informed that we needed to return to Calgary on Friday. Friday was about 100 days since his last chemo doses. When Bonita and I told Julian of the possibility that the two and half years of chemo had not achieved what we hoped, he was upset for a while, but then he looked up through tear filled eyes and asked, "When's supper?" Mom said, "Oh, we're a little late because of all this." Julian responded, "But I have to eat. I have a soccer game at 7:00." He had a bite and headed out to the soccer field; his team won 8 to 3 in the pouring rain and springtime hail. He came home, full of energy and pride, ice cold and exhilarated.

He went back to Calgary (2.5-hour drive) on Friday and had more tests done. Today, Tuesday, a week after the doctors' first suspicions, we were given the results. Julian's leukemia has relapsed. He will need to undergo intensive chemo for six weeks, followed by radiation therapy, followed by full body radiation and a bone marrow transplant (the last two if a suitable donor can be found). We are not sure how long he will be in ACH (Alberta Children's Hospital) but he may be away from home for four months. His treatment schedule will be much more vigorous than last time because the cancer that has presented itself is obviously "chemo resistant." Our son will walk a very difficult road in the coming weeks and months. The doctors are going to "push him to the wall." You might remember how many difficulties our son had: from diabetes to osteoporosis and peripheral paralysis and all sorts of other problems. The doctors are concerned that many of these same side effects will present themselves in the near future. They promise to be watchful.

Our family is deeply saddened by this development; we pour out our lament before the Lord: "How long, O Lord? How long?" (Job 3:23-26).

I had hoped that this journal had ended. It was not to be.

Pray for Julian, that he hold fast to the promises of God. Pray for his mother. Pray for his siblings. Pray for us all. Yes, pray for us all.

john & bonita; lorien, christopher, Julian, reuben and martin

Day 1065

Dear Family and friends

It has been more than six weeks now that the first suspicions arose and confirmation came that Julian's cancer had relapsed. We have been coming to terms with this great disappointment seeking and receiving strength from the Lord who watches over us. Julian has undergone extensive radiotherapy and chemotherapy for the past month and is now in a sort of "holding pattern." The treatments have once again brought the cancer into remission (i.e., no detectable measure of leukemic cells in his blood or bone marrow). Modern technology can test to the DNA level and there is no evidence of cancer in his body. This, however, does not give absolute certainty that there is not one single solitary cancerous cell in his body… and that is what must be achieved. That is what two and half years of chemo failed to achieve. He has not been subjected to all the complex side-effects that he endured last time. For this we are very thankful. He did not need to spend much time in the hospital but was discharged within ten days.

The medical team has recommended that Julian receive a bone marrow (BMT) or peripheral stem cell transplant (PSCT). A BMT infuses into the patient, bone marrow drawn from a donor's hip. In the marrow are found the stem cells which recolonize the patient's marrow and which produce the blood. A PSCT draws these same stem cells from the donor's blood instead of the marrow.

Julian is scheduled to receive a PSCT on August 18/19. For a transplant to succeed it is necessary to find a "matching donor." This means that the cells of the donor have a similar genetic structure to the patient. We are thankful to the Lord that two (!) of our sons [Christopher 17 and Martin 12] are perfect matches. (Not only do our sons look alike, in many other ways it seems they are identical!) Many patients in similar circumstances need to find an unrelated donor (and often are not successful). We are grateful to God that this is not necessary.

Last week, Christopher, the donor, was given the first of four injections to stimulate his bone marrow to produce an abundance of stem cells, which will then spill into his blood stream. These were "harvested" on Tuesday. He spent two nights and a day in the children's hospital.

On August 15, Julian will receive powerful chemotherapy drugs followed by three days of full body radiation to completely destroy his bone marrow. The stem cells harvested from Chris will be infused into his blood from where they are able to find their way back into the bone and create new marrow. The "graft" will take ten to twelve days to "take." During that time Julian's white blood cell counts will fall to zero and he will have no immune system functioning in his body. It is in that crucial time that Julian's life will be in God's hands in a special way. Any and every virus and bacteria can pose a potential life-threatening danger.

There is a song in Dutch: "We lay our children in your hands, O Lord." In our family we are learning to do that, and though the lesson is well taught, it is often hard learned. We had hoped in February, at the end of 30 months of treatments, that our son would not have to walk this road. But yet, we knew that this was a possibility. It does not make the heart ache less, however.

We know that in all things God works for good with those who love him: and this we do. This is our confession; this is our hope.

john & bonita; lorien, christopher, Julian, reuben and martin

PSCT Day Minus Two

Dear Family and friends

Chemo started on Sunday: it was awful. The anti-nausea drugs could not hold back the assault. For hours Julian was wracked with wretched pain. The drugs, Ondansetron and Gravol, brought on sleep; the puking kept him awake. This caused delirium and confusion. Over and over, he kept saying, "I don't think I like this very much" and "I don't feel very good." Half asleep, half awake, his temperature over 39'C, he called for his brothers, his mother, his sister. Over and over, nausea washed over him like waves. As I held his head up off the bed, I wept for my dear son. We thank the Lord that this was only one day, one afternoon.

Yesterday the high dose radiation began. [18mv x-ray, two 7-minute bursts, left side/right-side, twice daily for three days.... for those who care to know.] These treatments are given at the Tom Baker Cancer Center across the Bow River, a ten-minute ambulance ride away: back and forth four trips per day.

To prepare him for his treatments, Julian lies on a 50-cm wide bed (as wide as he is with his hands flat against his side). This bed has 50-cm high Plexiglas sides. Julian lies flat on his back and his body is then "packed" into this bed by two technicians who bury him with flat vinyl bags (15cm x 60cm) filled with Vaseline and powdered glass as well as larger bags filled with glass beads. These bags mimic the density of human tissue. Instead of the contours of the human body, these bags turn Julian into a 50 cm x 35 cm x 180 cm cubic object. That way he will get an even dose of radiation throughout his body. He is monitored with 8-10 electrodes taped to his body.

This whole procedure is rather bizarre. The bed in which he lays is a "home-built" contraption that the engineers in the maintenance department designed and built. (It looks ominously like a see-through coffin!) It is functional but definitely low-tech. With Julian buried in all this, the bed is wheeled into this brand new, incredibly high-tech room with the latest radiation and computer technology. The contrast between the bed and the x-ray machine is so striking it defies description. As Donna the technician said: "Total body irradiation is not an exact science." They place him against the far wall and the x-ray machine is turned towards him. The small cross that appears on your arm when you place it on the x-ray table now appears a large cross on his body! And then we all leave him in that room. The x-rays are too dangerous for us; if we stayed in the room we would be exposed to reflected rays. But Julian has a target on his body! The radiologist told us that the first dose of radiation was sufficient to cause death. Julian had twelve such treatments. Left side, right side, morning and afternoon, for three days.

After each session we see our son go lower and lower. He quit eating today. The chemo and the radiation treatments will cause all his mucous membranes to shed their outer layers and cause ulcers through out his digestive tract. The radiation causes his saliva glands (painfully) to quit functioning as well. [Loss of appetite is a blessing in a way, since it allows his system to shut down.] Tomorrow Julian will begin to receive all his nutrition through his central line. We hope and pray that nausea is not part of this. Lord, have mercy!

On Thursday, with his own bone marrow destroyed, the peripheral stem cells harvested from Christopher will be infused into his blood stream [PSCT]. And then the waiting begins... 10 days, 12 days, 14 days. Will the procedure work? Will the new cells "take?" Or will infection take over? Will his body recover? Will his strong healthy body reject the transplant? Without the cells from Chris, the chemo and radiation doses are fatal. We pray the Lord will preserve his life. We know he cares for us. We believe that not a hair is falling from his head without his Father willing it so... but who, who can understand his ways?

We have met with the physiotherapist, who will help Julian keep his muscle tone during his weakest times. We have met with the pharmacist who keeps us abreast of the drugs being used — today. We have met with the dietician who will help us to develop a low bacteria diet for Julian as well as the social worker who helps us contact relevant government agencies. The care team continues to get bigger and bigger. We have been warned that at any moment and with no notice Julian could be transferred to ICU. That should not cause us any alarm however [yeah sure!], but in ICU they are set up for more specific and constant monitoring. If Julian should develop an infection, then ICU is equipped to care for him. Julian's silver cord and golden bowl are very fragile (Ecclesiastes 12:6).

On the other hand, the doctors are very insistent that Julian be encouraged to go out on passes. We have taken up residence at a hotel where we can take him for a few hours of escape from his hospital room.

We lay our children in your hands, O Lord.

john and bonita; lorien, christopher, Julian, reuben and martin

PSCT Day Zero

Dear Family and friends

Julian received his transplant today. In a way, it was anticlimactic. Two small bags of stem cells from his brother Chris, a total of about 150 ml, were infused via his central lines into his blood stream. The whole process took 17 minutes. The bags were thawed in his room and infused immediately. There was the possibility of violent allergic reactions so the medical care team was in place, prepared for anything, but Julian mostly slept through the procedure. We did wake him so that he might remember the process.

Many transplant patients call Day 0 their "second birthday." I mentioned this to Julian the other day while waiting for the radiation therapy that was killing his bone marrow. He said,

"Yeah, I guess it's like being *born again!*" We had a good chuckle about the double entendre. We asked Dr. Alberts how the stem cells find the way back into the bone marrow? How can they "know" where they need to be, and how do they get from the blood stream, into the center of hard bones and start manufacturing blood. Dr. Alberts said, "It's magic!" He went on to say that there is much about the human body and its many functions that we do not understand. How stem cells take up residence in the long bones of the body is one of them!

Yesterday we received shocking news from home. Reuben, our next son, accidentally set himself on fire! He, with his younger brother and a friend, had gasoline and matches: a dangerous mix. They had dissolved Styrofoam in gasoline, added engine oil and created their own "Napalm." Attempting to start just a little fire they poured some on the lawn but the mixture exploded into flame and then leapt back to the bottle. The gasoline had been stored in our garden shed, and on a hot August afternoon was like more than 40'C. As they stomped on the fire, the plastic bottle holding their concoction turned into a Napalm flame-thrower… and Reuben was in the way. He was wearing shorts. The sticky burning mess stuck to his legs. He has first and second degree (and perhaps some third degree) burns from his ankles to the tops of his thighs covering 12%-15% of his body. He will remain in Lethbridge Regional Hospital for some time. The doctors will not be able to make a clear assessment of the damage to his legs until Tuesday. Then they will decide if he needs any skin grafts to repair some of the more seriously damaged areas.

Reuben is in relatively good spirits (though I am not sure about how good he felt when I arrived in his room tonight!) and is learning to master a wheelchair. He rolls about with both his legs straight out. Though his name was not mentioned and his face not shown, he made the local TV, radio and newspaper news as an object lesson for other children. Gasoline is not a plaything.

The greatest concern right now for Reuben is infection. The doctors take great care in ensuring that no infection invades any of his burns. We pray the Lord bless those efforts. One of the consequences of this accident is that Reuben may not come into contact with Julian. Reuben's wounds are a hot bed for infection and Julian must be protected from any infection. The two brothers (best friends) are now quarantined from each other. (It helps that they are separated by 220 km of prairie!) The doctors in Calgary were very quick in advising us to have Reuben transferred to the hospital Julian is in but we decided against that. The rest of our family needs as much stability and normalcy as possible. When we told the doctors that we decided to leave Reuben in Lethbridge because we needed life to be as normal as possible, they had to laugh. "You call this normal? This can't be considered normal by anyone!"

We thank the Lord that Christopher had the presence of mind to smother the flames and get Reuben into the shower and into a tub of cold water before calling 911. The cold water may have saved Reuben from much more serious injury. Someone said, "That Chris is a pretty special guy. He saved two brothers' lives within 24 hours! Does he have a halo?" Reuben, through his pain, kept repeating, "Don't tell mom and dad!"

Coaldale is a relatively small town and has a volunteer emergency response and fire department. Several of the volunteers are members of the church I pastor. I heard later that as they responded to the 911 call, one of them said, "That's close to our pastor's address! No, that is our pastor's address!"

As you can imagine our lives are rather stressful today. I came home to Coaldale via Greyhound Bus to care for Reuben, and Bonita stayed with Julian. We will switch duties next week. I just spoke to Bonita, and she tells me that Julian is doing quite fine. He recovered from all the "dopey" medicines and had a pleasant evening with his mom. Now the waiting begins... Lord, have mercy on our sons!

john & bonita, lorien, christopher, Julian, Reuben, and martin

PSCT Day 9

Dear Family and friends

It has been nine days since Julian received the stems cells harvested from his older brother Christopher. These have been very difficult days. Each day we saw our son go lower and lower. He just lies in his bed. He does not even want his hospital bed "turned up" a bit. He has six IV pumps hooked up to his two lines. One line is for his feeding: a solution of fats and amino acids. The other line accommodates (1) the solution of electrolytes and minerals he needs to survive; (2) the dextrose hydration solution to regulate his fluid balance; (3) the various meds and anti-nausea drugs; (4) the antibiotics; and (5) a morphine drip.

Julian is in constant pain. The radiation conditioning that he underwent 10-12 days ago has caused his mucous membranes from lip to gut to ulcerate. His GI tract is completely raw. He has eaten not much more than one slice of bread in the last two weeks. His mouth and throat are so sore he cannot speak above a whisper. He does not swallow but has a vacuum line to clear his mouth of skin and blood and saliva. There is one anti-nausea drug he takes orally. It takes him about a half hour to psyche himself up to swallow once. He controls his own morphine level and so he boosts it to three times above the baseline drip and receives a powerful tranquilizer to relax his esophagus in order to keep it from cramping up. Vomiting is a terrible experience as his stomach acids burn his raw flesh. He has a constant low-grade fever which is evidence of an infection of some kind. The doctors are treating that with the antibiotics but are unable to identify its source or location so they are attacking it with a broad spectrum of antibiotic and anti-fungal drugs.

When we look at our son so sick, we can only say that in the short term the cure is worse than the illness. We have not seen our son so weak in all the three years that he has fought this battle. (Monday is the third anniversary of his diagnosis.) But we do not lose heart. The doctors are encouraged with his progress and stamina. So many transplant patients fare much worse than our son. So many need to go to ICU. So many become terribly, terribly ill with fungal infections, fever, and diarrhea. When they see Julian, they see a strong healthy lad who has every advantage to go on to a full and complete recovery. I suppose it is a matter of perspective. And we are sure that the Lord is hearing the prayers of the saints, all of you, who lift up our son's needs before the Lord. I am sure that God is hearing your prayers for him and answering them with "Yes, I will do as you ask."

Dr. Alberts is confident that tomorrow or Monday will be the turning point. Julian's blood counts (the ones we are concerned about) have been at "zero" for some days now. After the radiation treatments they plummeted. His platelets (blood clotting agent) fell to ten percent of normal. He needs transfusions every second day. Somewhere out there is a platelet donor who is a close HLA (blood markers) match to our son. We do not know who or where, but this donor has been assigned to Julian. Because he needs so many transfusions, they try to use a single donor to reduce the possibility of reaction. When a patient receives multiple blood product transfusions, the possibility of allergic reactions rise. This risk is substantially reduced when there is a single donor. To think that there is one person who is diligently going to a donor clinic to help save our son's life is moving and humbling.

The blood supply of the Canadian Blood Service is low. This is because so many potential donors cannot answer the questions about lifestyle in a satisfactory way. Christians have an opportunity to make a powerful witness here. To be a safe donor today you need to be celibate or in a long term faithful monogamous heterosexual relationship. You also may not have had any new body piercings or tattoos in the past year. Not much of the world fits that description. This is an appeal to all of you to become regular blood donors and single donor platelet candidates.

Reuben came home yesterday. He now is an outpatient and needs to be at the hospital at 9:00 AM every day. This morning they did not put any dressings on his right leg. Things are progressing well for him though he still suffers much pain because of the burns on his other leg. It will be some time before all is well. He may not be able to attend the first days of school next week.

Last Sunday the brother-in-law of our oldest son, Shaun (recently married) died in a drowning accident in the Pembina River. Stan was buried on Thursday. As you can imagine Bonita and I feel stretched rather thin. Bonita was with Reuben in Lethbridge; I was in Calgary with Julian; our hearts were in Edmonton with Shaun and Juanita. Where are we needed? How can we be a support to all our children? How long, Lord, how long? Lord, how much? We are humbled under God's mighty hand, but yet we trust that he will lift us up in due time. We must learn again and anew to cast all our anxiety on him.

Today Julian asked his mother to bring her hair cutting scissors and a razor along to the hospital. His hair is falling out very rapidly. The next time I see him he will have that classic cancer patient's crown of glory. "Are not two sparrows sold for a penny? Yet not one of them will fall to the ground apart from the will of your Father. And even the very hairs of (Julian's) head are all numbered. So don't be afraid; (he) is worth more than many sparrows" (Matt 10:29 ff). Help me Lord, not to be afraid... not to be afraid.... Lord, remember that even the sparrows and swallows have a place in your presence (Ps 84:3); count Julian's hairs Lord. I believe! Help my unbelief!

john & bonita, Shaun & Juanita, lorien, christopher, Julian, Reuben & martin

PSCT Day 25

Dear Family and friends

Julian's transplant has taken hold. As the doctors had assured us, the first evidence that Julian's new bone marrow was functioning showed up on Day 12. They had said that his counts would rise from "zero" on Day 10 or 12. Right on schedule! We thank the Lord for answering your many prayers. But during that time Julian's mouth sores were really quite terrible. As soon as his "counts" began to rise his mouth began to heal and within a few days he was able to swallow again. His also able to speak again but his voice is still quite fragile. These past two weeks, since you have heard from us, have not been without challenges, however.

Julian developed severe pain in his stomach and gut. His

nausea and diarrhea became worse and worse. His fever rose to 40.9C (105.6F). At times delirium set in. Last Saturday (Day 17) he began to pass blood. The doctors became very concerned for him. On Sunday afternoon he was moved into ICU. Bonita called me very shortly before I had to preach. Though his life was not at immediate risk, the ICU team is better able to monitor his vital functions. The difficulty the doctors had was an inability to diagnose the cause of his problems, any error here and death would come quickly. I resolved to lead the worship service, in spite of this setback. I preached a sermon based on Lord's Day 1 of the Heidelberg Catechism: ***What is your only comfort in life and death?***

That I am not my own,
but belong with body and soul, both in life and in death,
to my faithful Savior Jesus Christ.
He has fully paid for all my sins with his precious blood
and has set me free from all the power of the devil.
He also preserves me in such a way
that without the will of my heavenly Father
not a hair can fall from my head; indeed,
all things must work together for my salvation.
Therefore, by his Holy Spirit
he also assures me of eternal life
and makes me heartily willing and ready
from now on to live for him[*].

---

[*] *Book of Praise*, op cit., 518.

I was sorely tested that day. Do I believe that confession to be true? Do I believe it to be true for me? That all things work together for my salvation? Can this be true for Julian? That not a hair can fall from his head outside the will of his heavenly Father? Am I assured of eternal life? For me? For Julian? For his mom? "I believe, Lord! Help me in my doubts: in my fears; help me Lord in my unbelief!"

After church I made the 220 km trip to the hospital, where Bonita and I met with the Internal Medicine Team and the Oncology Team. The Internal Medicine team said that there was no evidence that Julian had an infection other than a low-grade fever, and so the problem must be either the antibiotics (he was on five powerful antibiotic drugs) or Graft Versus Host Disease (GVHD). However, because of all the antibiotics in his body any sample taken for lab testing would come up negative.

GVHD is when the graft, being a new immune system, begins to attack the patient (the host). This is the very opposite of organ rejection in transplant patients. In that case the patient's immune system rejects the foreign object, the transplanted organ. In GVHD the transplant rejects the patient!

Julian's cancer doctors, however, saw no other evidence of GVHD and so they were quite sure that there was some infection somewhere. The standard treatment for GVHD is steroids. But steroids would aggravate an infection causing it to run out of control, which would risk Julian's life.

Withdrawal of the antibiotics, if there were an infection, could be disastrous. Not doing anything was not appropriate either. So the advice of the Internal Medicine team was "withdraw the antibiotics and treat the GVHD with steroids!" However, the Oncology team said, "double down on antibiotics and let's beat this infection!"

In the end the decision was left to us, Julian's parents. "You have to decide. What should we do?" As parents we had to make a life-or-death decision! What to do! How can we even make such a decision? We asked it we could have a bit of time to talk about our choices and to pray over this. Life and death hung in the balance. "You choose!" We did not know who was right and who was wrong, so after laying this before the Lord, we went back to the Care Team meeting and said to the Oncology team members, "We know you and we trust you, so we are going to go with your advice. We don't know the Internal Medicine team. Double down on antibiotics!" But Julian's doctors then said, "While you were gone the internal medicine team convinced us that we are wrong. We need to treat Julian with steroids." The doctors proceeded to withdraw the antibiotics, one drug per day, and instead administer steroids.

None of us slept well on Sunday night. Even Julian's doctor slept little, constantly checking on his patient. Dr. Alberts is an evangelical Christian. He was on call that night and slept at the hospital. He told me later that he spent most of the night on his knees in prayer, asking the Lord to bless his decision to change his mind. We thank the Lord that a correct diagnosis was made and the treatment had the desired effect. By Tuesday, Julian's fever had broken, his diarrhea was brought under control, his nausea lifted somewhat, and his smile (tentatively) returned. He went back to his ward on Thursday afternoon, his brush with death averted.

Monday had been my birthday. Lorien had been vacationing in Ontario and flew home in the evening. Shaun and Juanita arrived from Edmonton. The rest of us came from Coaldale. Even Reuben was with us. We "celebrated" my birthday around Julian's bed in ICU. The family sang "Happy Birthday" quietly, not to disturb the other children. We went out for dinner, but it seemed inappropriate to celebrate without our "middle son." And yet we can thank the Lord for each new day, each year that we have together as a family. We were able to speak to Shaun and Juanita about the drowning death of her brother. They, in the midst of sorrow, trust in God for grace to help in time of need. There are new mercies every morning. In the midst of crisis, change, anxiety, death, one thing never changes: the Lord is ever faithful.

By Friday, the doctors wanted Julian to leave the hospital on day pass. For a few hours each day he is freed from his IV pole and allowed to leave the hospital. He is not strong enough to walk so we take him out in a wheelchair, wrapped up in a blanket, mask on, hat pulled down, spirits up.

However, to watch this young athlete struggle to get out of a wheelchair and into the car is difficult for me. We head out to our hotel room, where he loved to just get into a bed and sleep undisturbed by nurses and doctors and pumps and people. Just sleep. He told me that he is sick and tired of being sick and tired. Often he is overwhelmed with exhaustion. When we asked the doctor about this, he assured Julian that this was "normal" for transplant patients. Julian (and we with him) needs to keep the long-term perspective. "It will take months to regain your stamina. Perhaps by Christmas you will feel normal again." At this, tears welled up in our son's eyes. Christmas seems such a long time from now. The doctor stressed that though the treatment does not appear very dramatic — some chemo, some radiation, a transfusion — we must keep in mind that Julian has had a transplant. He has had a very dramatic and significant procedure performed on his body, one that compares to any other kind of transplant. On top of that his body needs to recover from the "collateral damage" done by the radiation therapy. Fatigue, exhaust-tion, nausea: these are all normal responses.

Julian must begin to eat again. For twenty-six days he has eaten nothing. Now, his digestive system needs to wake up. We encourage him to have a few sips of ice water per day. A diet caffeine-free *Coke*, a few sips per day. A few ounces of fruit punch. A quarter slice of bread. Half a peach. Each day, each hour we need to encourage him to eat something, anything. The chemo and radiation and mouth sores, however, have stripped his mouth of taste buds. They take some time to heal. In the mean while all things taste "gross," as Julian says. As well, his stomach and brain are not synchronized and his stomach needs to learn its function again. Today Bonita made some home-made chicken soup. Julian managed his first meal since August 14. Toast, soup and a bit of a banana.

If things remain stable and Julian, under God's grace, continues on this road to recovery, he will be discharged as soon as he is able to maintain a caloric intake sufficient to sustain himself. That might take a week or so. If he is not able to eat enough, they will begin to feed him through a tube to his stomach. He still struggles with nausea.

When he is discharged, he will not be able to leave Calgary, however. He will remain an outpatient for two to three weeks, the doctors closely monitoring his progress. We anticipated that he would spend his 16th birthday (Sept 21) in the hospital but perhaps he will be an outpatient by then. We dare not yet look forward to the day that he returns home.

Reuben is recovering well from his burns. He spent ten days in the hospital and some more as an outpatient of the physiotherapy clinic. He now has only a few areas on one thigh that still need thrice daily attention. We thank the Lord that he has healed so well, so quickly. He will need to watch that he not get sunburn for the next few years. We are thankful, though, that Reuben was able to begin school on the first day. And as I wrote above, he too came to Calgary to visit Julian, not having seen him for more than three weeks, his quarantine now lifted.

Our family faces special challenges as we maintain two "homes." Bonita and I see each other twice a week as we trade places. Our routine is that she spends Saturday to Tuesday in Calgary. I drive up on Tuesday to relieve her and she goes home to Coaldale to care for the others. Back and forth we travel: 440 Km (280 M) round trip week after week. I estimate that I have made the trip more than 60 times in the 13 months that we have lived in southern Alberta. Together, Bonita and I have traveled this route 30 times (over 13,000 km / 8,000 mi) since Julian's diagnosis in early June. We also daily pray for safe journeys as we travel early mornings and late nights across the prairie landscape.

We thank the Lord for all of you who pray for our sons and our family.

john & bonita, Shaun & Juanita, lorien, christopher, Julian, Reuben and martin

PSCT Day 39

Dear Family and friends

We celebrated Julian's 16th birthday last week. In my last update I had indicated that we had hoped that he would be an out-patient by then. This was not to be. Even now Julian continues to be in the Children's Hospital. For Julian is simply unable to eat. For 43 days now (ever since his radiation treatments began) he has not had a decent meal. For the first few days that he was eating again, he managed to eat just a bit, but now he simply cannot keep anything down.

They had cut him off his IV nutrition in the hope that his appetite might be stimulated. This did happen. His taste buds have begun to function again, and his hunger has increased.

But he is unable to keep his food down. (Yesterday he was unable to keep down even three ounces of soup!)

Because of some of the drugs he is on he was losing almost a kilo (two pounds) per day. After eight days of that kind of weight loss they attempted to put in a NG tube (one of those awful things that go up your nose and down your throat.) The procedure was completely traumatic and terribly painful for our son. They had wanted to put in the day before his birthday, but he pleaded for them to hold off for a day. On the night of his birthday the first attempts were made but were unsuccessful. The next day under local anaesthetic the tube was inserted. The pump was started at 30 ml per hour. After four hours the nausea started and Julian ejected the line along with his nutritional supplement: total failure! The doctors have started his IV feedings again but this type of feeding is very hard on his liver. The only other options left are a nasal tube all the way to his small intestine or a surgically implanted tube, by-passing his stomach. Both of these kinds of tubes will mean that he no longer will be able to go out on passes... For now, he continues to attempt regular food twice a day.

Julian had to endure a "barium follow-through" where he had to drink three glasses of chocolate flavoured barium and then had to make repeated visits to x-ray so that the doctors could examine his GI tract. [You can imagine the struggle that was to keep inside!] They found no serious physical problem (blockage) to cause his inability to eat. It seems that his stomach is inflamed and swollen and simply cannot let food pass easily. Though Julian is not in immediate danger we are very concerned for his health. Because he is not eating, he is becoming frailer every day. Walking even a small distance is becoming more and more difficult. We may have to go back to using a wheelchair on passes.

We are thankful to the Lord that the stem cells graft is healthy and functioning well. Julian's blood counts, though they are up and down erratically, still usually fall within "normal." He needed a few transfusions to help him along the way but for the past ten days he has been holding his own. The doctors took a bone marrow sample at "Day 28" which showed no cancer at all. We thank the Lord that this part of Julian's procedure is a success so far. As Doctor Louis (in Ottawa) used to say: We have to beat the cancer, the rest is just a side show! I wonder how he would rate this eating problem "side show"? Is it a two or 3? Or would it be a 7 or 8?

Julian enjoys receiving your mail. There were birthday cards that came from around the world: cards and mail and email from friends and family and "strangers." He does not have much space in his room, so each day "yesterday's" cards go into the box to make room for "today's" mail. A real pleasure for him. At times however, he does not even have the energy to open your mail. Bonita or I sit beside him and tear open the envelopes and he then reads each one as he lies in his bed.

His school friends surprised him on the Saturday before his birthday. Some parents drove the whole lot of them to Calgary to throw him a party. They were in our hotel suite before Julian arrived on his pass. A good time was had by all. On his birthday, I drove his brothers and sister to Calgary for the afternoon. [Now we make the 450 Km round trip in an afternoon and evening!] We had a wonderful day together. It had been a long time since we were all together (my birthday two weeks ago doesn't count because Julian was in ICU and remembers little of the day). Recently, I preached in Calgary. One of the members there asked me what he could do for our family. I said that we so enjoyed the interaction with the professional players of the Ottawa sports teams at CHEO, and that there seemed to be no such relationship between ACH and the Calgary teams. He said he would take that on as a personal project. On the afternoon of Julian's birthday, two players from the Calgary Flames (the local professional NHL hockey team) came to visit Julian and gave him and his siblings autographed cards, with a hat and T-shirt for Julian. We got some pictures of their visit. A fun moment. Earlier the Calgary Stampeders (the local professional CFL football team) gave him an authentic "1998 Grey Cup Championship Game Ball" autographed by all the players in the 1998 championship team: Calgary!

In the midst of all this we wonder what each day will bring; what about this week? Next month? Ah, yes, the Lord teaches us, "Do not worry for tomorrow, for tomorrow will worry about itself." Yet, we wonder: Will there be progress, or will Julian continue to regress? Certainly, the past week has not been filled with great steps forward. Julian is becoming discouraged. One day as he was vomiting his latest attempt at supper, he was crying and muttering and angrily spitting into his bowl. It was the first time in three years that I saw him really angry about this all. It broke my heart. We can only wonder at the Lord's wisdom.

> Find rest, my son Julian, in God alone;
> our hope comes from him.
> He alone is your rock and salvation;
> He is your fortress; you will not be shaken.
> You salvation and honour depend upon God.
> He is your mighty rock, my son, your refuge.
> Trust in him at all times, Julian.
> I pour out my heart to him for you, my dear son.
> For God is our refuge
> - From Psalm 62

john & bonita; lorien, christopher, Julian, reuben and martin

Chapter Five

Through the Valley of Tears
PSCT Days 55-85

PSCT Day 55

Dear Family and friends

We had hoped that Julian would have been discharged by his birthday. Then we hoped that he would be home by his brothers' birthday (Chris 18 and Martin 13 on October2). Then we hoped that he would be home by Thanksgiving. We continue to hope.... Julian has battled nausea for many weeks now. His problem has gone from normal, to irregular, to unusual, to unprecedented. The doctors have never seen anything like this in their transplant patients. Moreover, every attempt to place an NG tube through his nose to his stomach has failed, with the tube being vomited up. As a last resort, the doctors planned to place a gastro-tube surgically bypassing the throat and esophagus and going directly into the stomach. This was not a preferred option, however, since the risks inherent in surgery and the risk of infection are high.

We wish to acknowledge publicly that an answer came to us via the REFNET!* Rev. Ralph Boersema formerly a missionary in Brazil, he is a faithful reader of these postings, and humbly suggested something based on his experience with starving children on the mission field. There they gave small amounts of food — even only a spoonful or less every half-hour or hour — to conquer the nausea related to empty stomachs. This advice resonated in Julian's mother's heart: food as the solution to nausea! Not more drugs or surgery! Since the last failed NG tube, we have been feeding Julian Gerber baby food in small amounts: a tip of a teaspoon. He has been able to keep this food down (mostly). Even his brothers, who came for a visit, were commissioned by their mom to get Julian to take a tiny bit of a teaspoon of baby food every half hour or so. One of the doctors remarked that our intestines have virtually no blood supply and that they get their nutrition via the nutrients that pass through the intestinal wall. Julian's intestines had gone dormant because of the lack of food, and so his stomach responded with nausea. Our introduction of tiny bits of food "woke up" his dormant gastrointestinal tract a fraction of an inch at a time.

Though he still struggles with nausea, especially in the

---

* The mailing list to which I posted this journal.

morning, he has made great gains in caloric intake in the past few days. The doctors are pleased; his parents are thrilled. Julian also needs to break out of his hospital "mind set." Though he wants to get out, he is in a sort of "embryonic comfort zone," with his IV pole as an "umbilical cord." He is afraid to leave the place, though he does not want to stay. He has been *habituated*! *Institutionalised!*

This past Thanksgiving weekend our family was able to be together in Calgary. Ladies of the congregation in Coaldale provided a Thanksgiving meal, which we took along to Calgary where Bonita was staying with Julian. We enjoyed a wonderful day together on Saturday, with Julian in our midst. When we sat at table, Julian did not join us in our repast but was with us anyway. When we asked around the table for the things for which we give thanks, one said "food and drink," another said, "family fellowship," another "that Julian could be with us and that for the first time in more than eight weeks we could share a meal together." Julian thanked the Lord for "his wonderful doctors." On Monday he was doing so well, we took him home to Coaldale for a 24-hour pass! He is back in Calgary right now, but if he continues to improve his food and drink intake, he could be discharged within the week! (We also are thankful to the Lord that Reuben has made a swift and complete recovery from the burns he received during his mid August "chemistry experiment"!)

There is, however, a darker side to all our joy. Robert died on

Saturday. He died even as we were celebrating our Thanksgiving. Robert had a BMT two weeks before Julian had his transplant. They shared a room back in June when they were both diagnosed as "relapsed ALL" Robert also struggled with all sorts of complications; they were just of a different sort from Julian. Last week he was diagnosed with non-Hodgkin's Lymphoma, which was stres-sing his heart and lungs. On Monday he struggled with breathing. On Saturday, he passed on from this world. Robert spent the past ten weeks in Q1 and Q4. Julian has been in Q2. Because of privacy issues, doctors and nurses may say little about other patients. Robert had been moved to ICU but kept his bed on the ward. On Monday I noticed that his room was empty; none of Robert's things were there; no evidence that he had ever been there. I had to ask, "How's Robert?" Only then, was I told. When I told Julian he was stunned, he sat on his bed and shook for a while. Just a week ago we had met Robert and his mom in the hallway as one was going out on pass, the other coming back: two teens in wheelchairs, now acquaintances on similar journeys. Julian's first verbal response however, was, "I don't think that Mom will take this very well."

When Robert left Q1, Susanna joined us next door. Susanna (5) is a Down's Syndrome / Fetal Alcohol Syndrome / ALL patient. She is an Inuit child adopted by a Calgary family. Susanna has been moved to ICU. She has not been doing well. Big Josh (16), who has had his leg amputated above the knee because of bone cancer, has relapsed in his lungs. He has gone home to die. Little Josh (4) has had his AML (another kind of leukemia) relapse. His cancer has proven stubborn and the doctors have not been able to achieve remission. He will likely go to Cincinnati this week for some experimental drugs in one last attempt to save his life. Little Fosta (8 months) was *born* with cancerous tumours! After three failed attempts with chemo the doctors amputated her arm; we, with her young mother, wait with bated breath. Katie (15) has gone home after her chemo treatments for the same diagnosis as Big Josh; lung relapse after leg amputation. All around us every day, we face death and sorrow. New patients come in and we see the stunned looks on frightened faces. We are now the veterans in this battle. We hear of diagnoses: brain tumour, Wilm's Tumour, ALL, AML, bone cancers, the list goes on and on. We are now the ones who must go to the funerals to weep with the broken hearted. We mourn with parents who grieve the death of children; a sorrow inexpressible — a sorrow of shattered dreams and dashed hopes, of failed expectations and challenged faith. Cancer is the number one killer disease of North American children. Only traffic accidents / drowning claims more young ones. And we with Julian live in the midst of this sorrow. Our joy at his imminent discharge is tinged with sorrow for those whose discharge from Q-Cluster (the Oncology Ward at Alberta Children's Hospital) is much quieter; for those who exit via ICU, never to return to that busy place of hope and joy, of pain and sorrow.

I printed out the postings of the past several months and shared it with the nursing staff. One of the night shift nurses was reading it and asked what "Baca" was, or where. I said that this came from Psalm 84 where Baca's vale is both the place of sorrow and of hope for Christians on pilgrimage.

Dr. Barens, overhearing this, said, "You must be speaking of this place: Q-Cluster." Yes, the cancer ward is Baca's valley, a dry and weary place that yet is full of hope and joy; of battles joined, of victory won, but which often is the place of Rachel's weeping (Matthew 2:18). Here we journey through the valley of the shadow of death. This is a place where comfort seems so far away for many who must journey there, but...

> How blest are those whose strength thou art,
> Who on Thy ways have set their heart —
> The highways to thy habitation.
> For them refreshing fountains flow
> When they through Baca's valley go,
> A land of drought and desolation.
>
> The wilderness, with showers blest,
> Becomes for them a vale of rest.*

john & bonita; lorien, christopher, Julian, Reuben and martin

---

* Psalm 84:3, *Book of Praise,* op cit., 210.

PSCT Day 63

Dear Family and friends

Today marks nine weeks since Julian received his transplant: 63 days! It was 68 days ago that he was admitted to Alberta Children's Hospital to begin this course of treatment. Yesterday he was discharged. Today we came home from Calgary. This past week Julian has undergone a transformation. Just Thursday he was struggling to keep down even baby-food, though he was managing to do so. By Tuesday he was eating full course meals. Julian must now regain the 20 kg that he lost, but that should not be too difficult. He also needs to regain his physical strength. We thank the Lord that he answered the prayers of so many friends and family members. Even the doctors are impressed by his swift turnaround. They were a little nervous in letting this lad leave Calgary. Home is two and a half hours away. We insisted, however, that though they thought 220 Km (140 miles) was far, it was a lot shorter for us who have traveled that highway so many times! We were reminded many times yesterday and today that if there were any problems to phone immediately: we promised repeatedly to do so.

With respect to his transplant, Julian is doing remarkably well. He has not had any secondary problems of infections, pneumonia or other illnesses. The Graft Versus Host Disease is under control and the cancer itself has not recurred. It was only his digestive system that was unable to recover from the trauma of radiation and chemotherapy.

Thank you for the many prayers for Julian and for us all. The Lord has sustained us through these last two very difficult months. He has done that also through your prayers and encouragement as well as by your letters, cards, and calls.

We now begin on the next stage of this journey. He is still immune compromised because of his recent transplant and because he takes immuno-suppressant drugs to keep any rejection under control. Julian still needs to take great care in avoiding any risk of infection and infectious disease. He may not be in crowds: malls, restaurants, school or church. This of course will be difficult for a 16-year-old (for who can be more social than a 16-year-old?) School will be difficult, for he will need to work on his own, while his classmates and brothers work at school just down the block. Each day will bring on new challenges. Yet, each day we know that the Lord will provide new blessings for there are new mercies every morning: Great is your faithfulness, Lord, unto us.

From here we will need to develop new normals, new routines. We wonder what the Lord has in store for tomorrow, but he teaches us to cast our anxieties on him, for he cares for us. This he has demonstrated richly these past two months.

Praise and thank the Lord with us!

john & bonita, lorien, chris, Julian, reuben, martin.

PSCT Day 85

Dear Family and friends

It has been nearly three months now since Julian underwent his chemo and radiation conditioning – three months since his transplant. You'll remember how he was unable to eat for days and weeks and how you all prayed that there might come an end to his nausea. The Lord did hear and answered your prayers with "Yes." Julian has been home now for some weeks. We have been making thrice weekly visits to Calgary for follow up care in the oncology clinic. (In the past two months we have driven 14,500 kilometers [9,000 mi.] back and forth to the hospital).

Soon after his discharge from the hospital he contracted a virus (CMV) which most North Americans carry. This virus is harmless for the general population but is "opportunistic" for those with suppressed immune systems: transplant patients, cancer patients, AIDS patients. This virus can cause pneumonia, liver disease, and intestinal infections. Pneumonia is the most serious for it can develop as a serious acute illness.

Over the past years, medical technology has been able to refine its search for viruses to the point that it can count individual viruses per 200,000 white blood cells. CMV infection over 100 is dangerous; over 50 the warning flags go up; over 10 demands close follow up. Julian's virus counts have been hovering between 7 and 78 for the past weeks. This caused some consternation. Julian's Cancer doctors, in consultation with the adult transplant team at Foothills Medical Center, recommended that we not treat with antiviral drugs. On the other hand, the Infectious Diseases doctors, in consultation with the transplant team at Toronto Sick Children's Hospital, recommended that treatment proceed... and we were left with the choice of what to do. The anti-viral drugs would have suppressed cell production in his new bone marrow and would have created the need for all sorts of blood transfusions, and at its worst could have compromised the graft and caused bone marrow failure. On the other hand, the infection could develop into CMV pneumonia for which there is no known effective treatment.

We followed the recommendations of Julian's Cancer doctors and with fear and trembling took him home. Twice we have returned with him to Calgary on non-clinic days to admit him to hospital for fear of the onset of viral illness. Both times, he was soon returned home. Julian continues to do well, though he still has some drug related nausea and stomach pain. We hope and trust that he will soon be weaned from his drugs and go on to live a full and healthy happy life. His viral counts are very low, his weight is up, his spirits good, our visits to Calgary much less often.

As we reflect on these past weeks and months, we see that the Lord has been gracious and generous in his love for us. He has shown this also through the love and care of his people who have carried us to the throne with their prayers, encouraged us with words, supported us in deeds. May God bless you all for your kindness shown to our son and to us all. We thank the Lord for all of you. We covet your prayers; intercede without ceasing, not only for Julian, but for all who are burdened by the brokenness of this world.

This journal will once again be posted much less often. As life returns to a "new normal" we hope and pray that through this difficult procedure Julian has been cured of his cancer. We have traveled through the Valley of Baca (Psalm 84), but as someone wrote to us: Even from there we can see the hills (Psalm 121). We know that we still need new mercies every morning. We need grace for each new day. But in all this we have experienced beyond measure that the Lord is faithful, good and gracious – and his grace has been sufficient for us.

john & bonita; lorien, christopher, Julian, reuben and martin

Chapter Six

From Strength to Strength

PSCT Days 140-434

PSCT Day 140

Dear Family and friends

We went to Calgary today, to the Children's Hospital for Julian's first regular check up of the new year. He is doing very well. Dr. Rooda told him to start reducing his anti-rejection drug dosage by 1/5 per week until he is off completely. By February DV he will be free of this drug. It is the one that made him so sick from August to October and with which he still struggles. He will be glad to be rid of it! (Last week, one morning, he missed a dose. He could not figure out why he felt so good!) We don't need to return to Calgary for a regular visit for four weeks! (Quite a difference from going three times per week). His blood counts are good. He has avoided all the cold and flu bugs that we all seem to get, no pneumonia. He even has had his first haircut since August!

Julian is talking about going back to work and school. He is gaining weight. He is planning to get out to Ontario this summer. It is wonderful to be able to make plans again (under the condition of James, of course.) For months, we have not planned for more than a few days. Usually plans went no further than the next trip to Calgary. As that window becomes bigger, new horizons are opening and we look with confidence to the summer and beyond.

When we reflect on the past six months, we see how God has been good to us. He has taught us again and again that he is faithful and that he cares for us. We do not know what lies ahead for us or for Julian. Ten months ago, he went off treatment and we stepped out into an uncertain future. Today we again face an uncertain future. What will the Lord set on our path? We know that Julian has many hurdles to cross; he has many difficult health issues that he will need to overcome in the coming years but yet he is in good cheer, confident and happy. One thing is certain: He is a child of God, confident and happy in the Lord his God.

Together, in the darkness, we have seen the beauty of the stars.

john & bonita, lorien, christopher, Julian, reuben and martin

PSCT Day 196

Dear Family and friends

Julian went skiing today! Downhill skiing! (Well, snowboarding, actually.) We could not have imagined this possible four months ago. Last fall, he was so terribly ill we feared for his life. With him, we have looked death in the face. So many of his comrades have a different story. A different ending.

Joshua — "Big Josh" — died at 16. Last summer I sat with him late in the night, both of us unable to sleep, at Ronald Mcdonald House. He told me of all his friends who had died. "Fifteen," he said, "in the past year." He is now among those who have lost their battle. I wrote to you of the little girls who were born with cancer. Fosta and Emma. Two darling children. Two little girls born inside a month of each other, both in Calgary, both with a very rare cancer. Fosta had her arm amputated in a desperate attempt to save her life. Emma's tumor was like a monster with tentacles that moved in from her arm and wrapped itself around her spine. Fosta and Emma both died last week, within a day of each other. Both died before their first year was over. Morgan died too. We live with death as a constant companion.

And then there is "Little Josh." "Big Josh" and "Little Josh" are both from Lethbridge, just a dozen kilometers down the highway from our house. Josh and Josh were special friends. Little Josh is four years old and has leukemia. There was no hope for him. In October, while Julian was so ill, Big Josh was sent home to die, and Little Josh was sent to Cincinnati for one last try: a new experimental drug. I saw Little Josh on Wednesday. He is doing well. The new drug worked. His ALL went into remission; he had a transplant and is gaining ground and health daily. We saw him in Clinic wearing Big Josh's Nike cap! A special parting gift from one friend to another.

But what of Julian? Last month he told his doctor he wanted his life back, so Dr. Edwards told him to "Go! Get a life!" And he did! He has gone back to school, to church, to Bible study. He plays hockey, plays badminton, has gone snowboarding, chops firewood, and is ready to take on the world! This past Wednesday we went back to Calgary for a regular monthly check up. We were a little concerned, however, that Julian was not feeling really well. The clinic doctor for the month,

"Dr. Max" (Mad Max, someone once called him) looked at him and said incredulously, "Helloooo!! You've had a transplant, you know! You're playing hockey(!) at six months post transplant and you're concerned that you're tired! What do you expect?" He is going to set up an appointment with a sports medicine doctor to see if we can build a program for Julian to rebuild his stamina and strength. When we were leaving the clinic on Wednesday one of the nurses commented on how when they had checked his chart about the last visit, Dr. Edwards had simply written his report: *Get a life!* And Julian has. The medical team sees Julian as a wonderful and amazing success. Most children at six months post transplant are still fighting all sorts of complications. Julian has made an amazing turn around: God hears and answers your many prayers.

However, we live with the constant realization that death stalks cancer patients. Each change in Julian's appearance or well being brings thoughts of relapse. We do trust that God can preserve our son's life, but we know that there are other outcomes. And we need to know and remember and be reminded that in all things nothing will separate Julian or us from the love of God.... And yet we fear death. We fear relapse. For so many, there is no cancer victory. We remember Big Josh, Robert, Morgan, Emma, Fosta and all those who loved them and who have become our friends. We will never in a lifetime forget Fosta, smiling, beaming joy, waving her arm with no hand. We will remember Emma, quiet Emma. We will remember their mothers and the silent pain they bore each day as they agreed to heroic interventions to save their daughters', their babies' lives, to no avail. We remember Big Josh, an only child, his parents bereft of their pride and joy. Robert a youngest child; Morgan a beautiful girl. We are reminded that cancer has become the number one killer disease of children in Canada and the USA. Still, for Julian there are great victories. He lives his life with gentle joy, with peaceful passion, with quiet confidence in God. At sixteen, he is so grown up and yet just a boy.

I remember so vividly that day (it seems an eternity ago) that we had to tell Julian that his road to recovery might be three or four years. He said, "That's nearly till the next Olympics!" (The Summer Games just over in Atlanta) He could not imagine something that far away. And here we are 3½ years later: Still recovering!

May God bless our son.

Under the Mercy

john & bonita, lorien, christopher, Julian, reuben and martin

PSCT Day 278

Dear Family and Friends

It has been nearly a year since Julian's leukemia relapsed. It has been an eventful year. A year filled with fears and tears, with frustration and consolation. Yet it has been a year blessed by the Lord, who watches over us. One year ago, Julian was a healthy, robust teen enjoying the end of his chemotherapy. We could not imagine that he was not well.

Today he again is playing soccer in the community league. He is catching up on schoolwork. He is determined that he will be caught up to his classmates by the end of term. (He only began schoolwork in earnest in February!) What events have transpired this passed year!

Last week we visited the clinic in Calgary for his regular

follow up visit. He was given the "all clear" and need not return until mid August. This will be the longest stretch of time between clinic visits since August 30, 1996. We are thankful that we need not return as often. (You'll remember that we were going three times per week; now once in three months.) And so, under God's grace and providential care our lives are returning to normal. Dr. Roodal said, "Come back in August, for a pat on the back!" He is off all medication except for an anti pneumonia drug (two days per week). Julian, however, did come down with the flu earlier this month. He was really quite ill, but has been able to fight it off without any medical intervention. His brothers, who also were sick, shook it off in a day or two. Julian took a week to recover, but he did it on his own (so to say). Under God's blessings his immune system was able to fight back the virus.

We read in Romans 5:2,3 that Paul says, "We rejoice in our hope of sharing the glory of God. More than that, we rejoice in our sufferings, knowing that suffering produces endurance, and endurance produces character, and character produces hope and hope does not disappoint us..." Julian is living testimony to the truth of this passage. He has learned endurance. He has developed "character." Throughout all this we have had hope, a hope that does not and has not disappointed. For we hope in God. Julian too, in all of this, has striven to keep his mind fixed on things above.

We do not know what God has in store for Julian or for us.

The "window" of high risk is two years. He is only one third the way. Last time he only made 100 days "off treatment." He is now 265 days past "engraftment." We entrust him to our Father's care.

We thank the Lord and you for your support and prayers these past four years. We have seen a light shining in a dark place: the bright Morning Star (2 Peter 1:19; Revelation 21:16b).

We walk in the light of life (Psalm 56:13).

john & bonita, lorien, christopher, Julian, reuben and martin

Four Years Post-Diagnosis

Dear Friends of Julian

We spent three days in Calgary with Julian visiting various clinics at the Children's Hospital. He also had a bone marrow aspiration taken. When all was said and done the doctors said that his blood, marrow, lungs, and heart are all healthy. He can simply get on with his life with no restrictions in activity or environment. He need not return for further follow up till February. (Today is four years since his diagnosis!) We also thank you all for your prayers, support and love that you have had for us. Please continue to pray that the Lord will ensure that Julian's cancer not return and that he might go on from here to live a full and happy life.

john & bonita, lorien, chris, Julian, reuben and martin

PSCT 14 Months

Dear family and friends of Julian

Last Saturday evening we discovered a rash on Julian's back. We suspected shingles (a herpes zoster virus infection of the nervous system). It was late, but we called the hospital in Calgary. After some consultation the doctors agreed with our assessment and told us to come to Calgary immediately; don't wait for tomorrow. Greatly disappointed, Julian and I packed our bags and headed out on the highway just before midnight. We arrived at the children's hospital at two AM. By the time we had been processed through emergency and Julian was in a room it was 4:15 AM. The hospital supplied me with a cot and we got a few hours rest.

For the past three days the rash has been advancing down the main nerve on his left arm. Today, however, it seems that the infection has been halted. Julian is being treated with powerful antiviral drugs. Shingles is a scourge for these children. They develop this infection because they are immunosuppressed and still carry the virus from childhood. This is the same virus that produces chickenpox in children. For transplant patients, shingles, left untreated, is a very serious disease. If it invades the central nervous system, or sensitive nerves (e.g., the optic) significant damage can occur.

Julian remains in isolation in the children's hospital. He may not leave his room for fear of spreading the virus to other children. Because he is not really feeling ill, he is rather bored. (When he was really ill, he slept for days and weeks on end.) The doctors are confident that this is not a sign that his immune system is failing and that this is not a symptom of cancer relapse. All other signs demonstrate that Julian is a healthy teen. For this we give thanks and praise to the Lord. As you could imagine, there were a few fearful hours as we awaited Monday's lab results from his blood tests. If the infection has been halted (we will see tomorrow) then he should be able to come home by the weekend.

We thank the Lord for your continuing prayers and support.

john & bonita, Julian and siblings

PSCT Day 434

Dear family and friends of Julian

Julian returned home today. He is in good spirits and feeling well. The doctors are pleased with his good health.

We thank the Lord for new mercies every morning.

john & bonita, Julian and the rest

Chapter Seven

Awaiting the Final Day

Days End

Dear Family and friends

I've lost track of what day I should enter above my journal. I could calculate it but for some reason, it seems so unimportant. I suppose that's because of the funeral I attended yesterday. "Little Josh" died on Thursday. He was four years old. During the time that Julian was in the hospital in the fall and winter of 1999 we became friends with the families of the others in Q-Cluster. There were those, of course, who passed through the unit for a few days with a minor crisis or for maintenance chemo, but with the others, the newly diagnosed, the seriously ill, we built strong bonds. Little Josh was the last one still alive. All the others have succumbed to their illnesses. Robert and Morgan; the little babies, Fosta and Emma; Big Josh, Katie, Susanna, and now Little Josh; the list goes on: of them all, only Julian remains.

Little Josh was a Taiwanese baby adopted by a childless couple in Lethbridge. Devout Christians, they are members of the Presbyterian church. Little Josh was diagnosed when he was two years old. He valiantly fought his battle against leukemia. He relapsed time and again. He endured endless chemo, transplants, more chemo, experimental drugs; he nearly died numerous times. With unfailing hope in God, his parents and his congregation, his friends, prayed for little Joshee. Each time he was snatched from the brink of death. But in the end, though free of cancer, he died during a blood transfusion, his little body simply unable to withstand another medical procedure.

The funeral service was poignant, touching, grief filled. The readings were from Isaiah 40 and 60; among the songs were Joshee's favorites: "Jesus Loves Me, This I Know" and "Let Your Little Light Shine." There was acknowledgement of Joshua's baptism, of his simple love for Jesus, of his personal prayers for healing, of the faith of a four-year-old boy. The minister pointed us to the promises of God made to Joshee and to all who believe in Jesus Christ. But in it all there was a recognition that there are no clear answers to the questions that rise in our minds: how to make sense of this all? The brokenness of this world was set in sharp relief. The grace of God was set in bright contrast to the darkness of our sorrow as a family friend recounted how time and again, in times of great crisis, Joshee was carried through on the prayers of God's people and yet how in the end death came so swiftly during a rather routine procedure. Now we must look forward to the certain hope of the resurrection.

Other parents, whose children have died, were there too. Every funeral is also attended by staff from the Children's Hospital: always a doctor, a nurse, clinic staff, a social worker; they always come. We grieve together. Those whose lives are marked by childhood cancer, parents, families, medical staff, come to know each other well. The doctors and nurses are more than just that. They become our friends, the children love them, they love the children... and they come, each time, each time, to the graveside of another one. How do they manage?

I stood at Joshee's graveside with the Warners, the parents of "Big Josh." A year and a week ago we stood, not twenty feet away, at his open grave. Now grass covers the plot, a headstone marks the spot. We walked over together: the Warners and me. Josh too was an only child. It was beautiful bright & sunny, but it did not seem to be that way. Though there was no wind nor cloud, and the sun was strong, I felt a cold chill. What words can we use to bring comfort? What message is there that will suffice? In silence we waited for God; our hope is from him alone; from him is our salvation (Psalm 62). Two families, laying to rest their only children, their only sons, and we have five! Joshee's dad prayed at the graveside, and asked the Father in heaven, who gave up his only Son for us, that He might grant the strength needed to give up theirs. I cannot imagine the sorrow.

So many children have died: among our friends only Julian remains. Our joy and thankfulness to the Father for his good health is often marked by profound sorrow when we remember all those who have lost their loved ones, their children, their little ones, to cancer.

Striving with unwavering hope, straining our ears to catch the first sounds of the trumpet of God, and of the archangel's call (1 Thessalonians 4:16-18). We go from strength to strength till each of us appears before our Savior God in Zion.

john & bonita, lorien, christopher, Julian, reuben and martin

Postscript

That first Sunday, in Ottawa, our friend and elder Rob Speijer read a sermon on the first sign of the Messiah, when the Lord Jesus turned water to wine. That sermon had been prepared by my brother George, who was minister of Taber. He spoke of the super-abundant joy that the Lord Jesus brings into this broken world.

The first Sunday after Julian's initial treatments were completed, the new minister of Taber, Theo Lodder, preached in Coaldale, where we are now members. His text was about the first sign of the Messiah, when the Lord Jesus turned water to wine! He spoke of the Lord's grace! Our lives have been "bracketed" by this gospel of joy and grace.

We thank the Lord for all of you who faithfully prayed for our son and our family. I know that many of you have prayed for me that I might be able to continue to preach the gospel with boldness and clarity in the midst of this struggle. When Julian was diagnosed that August afternoon, I had preached

10 sermons of a planned 12 sermon series on Job. I wrote the last two on my laptop in the hospital at Julian's bed side.

In the second last one I wrote:

> Job had said, "Though he slay me, yet I will trust in him." Job's friends saw suffering in the light of sin and punishment. But God shows us that suffering is the opportunity for grace - an occasion for grace.

God's grace has been sufficient for us.

The battle is not over; the journey not finished; though there are many difficult days, only when it is dark can we see the stars.

www.ingramcontent.com/pod-product-compliance
Lightning Source LLC
Chambersburg PA
CBHW050328010526
44119CB00050B/720